Kamesh Goyal, Chairman Digit Insurance

I recommend this book by Robin if you want to learn how insurers can keep up with the changing customer preferences as customers go digital. It offers practical advice for insurance offerings to meet the needs of tomorrow's customers.

Brett King, Bestselling Author of The Rise of Technosocialism and Host of The Futurists podcast

In Attention Hacking, Robin takes inside the mind of a successful influencer applying his skillsets to the corporate and retail environments. From Crocodile Dundee analogies to Digital Scaling methodologies, this book is a trove of great case studies and hacks that will enhance your brand and engagement in the emerging 21st century marketplace

Rob Galbraith, CEO of Forestview Insights, Insurtech Influencer

"Breaking through is hard to do - unless you read Attention Hacking by noted expert Dr. Robin Kiera! The practical ideas and techniques Robin shares in this book will save you thousands on promotions and help you reach your intended audience in the most impactful way possible."

Sabine VanderLinden, "The Insurtech Queen"

I remember a quote I read on LinkedIn over five years ago, which I still use today when explaining the power of social media engagement. Commercial organizations are paying great attention to new B2B sales and marketing trends. Indeed, today over 75% of those commercial buyers use social media to be more informed about suppliers. They also complete 57% of their due diligence process before reaching out to a vendor for the very first time.

In this book, Dr. Robin Kiera dives into an important topic that many of our analytical and rational colleagues within insurance and finance forget. People buy from people. They buy from people they like. Likeness today is achieved through social proofing, commending authority, and applying the rule of scarcity. This means that bringing attention to a brand's values is more than necessary. It is a pre-requisite. Robin unveils the practical tools and techniques businesses must master to build authentic brand advocacy in the digital age. A must-read!

Eric Fulwiler, CEO of Rival

"The hardest and most important skill for any modern marketer is understanding how to find and earn the attention of their audience. This book is the BIBLE for making that happen in FS."

"Anyone looking to grow a brand and business in digital needs to read this book. The tips and advice will change the way you think about modern marketing."

"Robin is one of our generation's most brilliant marketing minds. Attention Hacking gives away all his secrets!"

"If you think digital marketing could be doing more to grow your business, this book is a MUST read."

Kobi Bendelak, CEO at InsurTech Israel

Great book and great author, Dr Robin Kira succeeds in providing professionals in the insurance and finance industry with the means and tools to increase contact points with customers and leads by using digital content on relevant channels.

Besides technical tips and advice the book is designed to provide also motivation for people and companies for whom Social and Digital Media does not come naturally.

Richard Sachar, CEO Investor Networks & Director Fintech Global

"This book is full of essential insights for senior insurance executives from one of the industry's leading digital insurance experts".

Richard Sachar, CEO, FinTech Global

"Robin's insights are a must-read for anyone who wants to know what creates marketing success in the insurance industry"

"Robin is one of the sharpest and most compelling thinkers in the insurance industry. This book is essential reading for industry professionals"

"Essential insights for insurance professionals written in Robin's inimitable clear, compelling and inspiring style"

"Robin Kiera explains clearly how attention hacking can outperform traditional approaches to marketing and customer experience as digital transformation redefines the insurance industry"

"In the new world of digital insurance, old approaches don't work. Robin Kiera analyses and explains what's required to reach customers much more effectively"

Denise Garth, Chief Strategy Officer at Majesco

In today's market there is so much noise to fight through and uncertainty on where the insurance market is heading, that influencer and content marketing through attention hacking can cut through the noise to educate, engage and develop a level of trust through a multi-channel approach. But it takes forward-thinking and thought-provoking content that is valued, consumed and establishes trust that by working with you and using your products they will see value both today and in the future. Robin's book synthesizes these concepts to help companies plan and execute relevant initiatives that can drive long-term value, engagement and results. As a fellow InsurTech influencer, I see the ~~postive~~ positive impact of these ideas each and every day!

Attention
Hacking

Attention Hacking

The Power of Social Media Selling in Insurance and Finance

Dr Robin Kiera

WILEY

Library of Congress Cataloging-in-Publication Data
Hardback: 9781394189052
ePDF: 9781394189069
epub: 9781394189076

Cover Design: PAUL MCCARTHY
Cover Image: GETTY IMAGES: © TUOMAS LEHTINEN
SKY10056337_092823

For Katja, Klara-Elisabeth, Karl-Hendrik,
and Johanna

Contents

Foreword by Julian Teicke

In extreme situations, you really get to know someone. I first got to know Robin when he initiated mediation in the legal dispute between Wefox and Lemonade, which was critical to Wefox's existence. With his help, we settled all the disputes without the need for lawyers. Robin, as an internationally renowned insurance expert and influencer, did not have a hidden agenda. His perspective was that a dispute like that only harms innovation in the industry and must be settled. As if it was the most obvious thing, he mediated for weeks and then finally led a marathon meeting between me and the Lemonade CEO. Together, the three of us were able to achieve the minor miracle of resolving the dispute.

While one cannot accuse Robin's keynote speeches or articles of shying away from provocative theses, one must see them – like this book – in light of the motivation to positively impact the insurance industry and push it toward innovation. You need to embrace innovation and be prepared to change to move with the times.

We also put this into practice at Wefox. In addition to direct sales, we rely on physical agents (brokers, tied agents, untied agents, underwriting agents) to ensure customer satisfaction. We believe that many things are possible through technology, but it is no substitute for interpersonal communication. As a digital full-stack insurance company, we see the innovation potential of the industry, in particular in risk avoidance through technology.

Board members, marketing and sales managers, and agents can learn three things from this book:

- Changes in communication and buying behaviour are unstoppable. We are not at the tail end of digitalisation; on the contrary, we are at the beginning. Now is the latest time for starting.
- Customers' attention is limited, whereas the supply of information is almost unlimited. Those who do not manage to establish themselves in the day-to-day world of their customers will lose their customer interface.
- The digital communication revolution has led to a collapse of the entry barriers for the production of content for customers. On the one hand, this has meant intense competition for customers' attention. On the other hand, however, it has led to enormous opportunities for new, smaller and medium-sized players. Today, smaller organisations can gain a disproportionate presence in the market.

Robin's book, *Attention Hacking*, is an abstract guideline for the actions of insurers in the digital world. It also contains many concrete recommendations and tips for beginners and professionals.

Julian Teicke
Founder and CEO of Wefox Berlin
May 2023

Foreword by
Dr Stefan Knoll

R obin Kiera is an impressive character. First of all, he is an academic and wrote his 500-page doctorate thesis on German military officer and politician Otto Philipp Braun.

I chose this introduction to highlight that Dr Kiera did not need to be entrepreneurial from an educational point of view alone. The latter, in particular, inspires me. Becoming an entrepreneur is a question of attitude, and if one is also successful, it is proof of one's personal ability to perform.

I met Dr Kiera when we converted Deutsche Familienversicherung into an Insurtech and wanted to list it publicly.

Dr Kiera assisted me in this process and was also at my side during several appearances, including in the United States.

When we founded Deutsche Family Insurance in 2007, digitalisation was not yet an issue, at least not like it is today and certainly not in the insurance industry. However, recently with the coronavirus pandemic, it has become clear that entrepreneurs who do not master online sales as an alternative or supplementary distribution channel have substantial challenges in selling their products or services. Before the coronavirus pandemic, customer behaviour changed gradually, and once the pandemic started, customer behaviour changed rapidly. Customers appreciate the ease of ordering online and the convenience of getting information on the Internet, and this needs to be considered by businesses.

With Dr Kiera, we utilised Alexa as a distribution channel. Even though sales results to date with Alexa are still relatively modest in scope, using Alexa for sales purposes implies the requirement of a somewhat superficial level of expertise: insurance products can be so simple that they can be sold via a voice assistant.

If state regulation – the unchecked urge for bureaucracy as a stop-gap solution for continuation of state failure at the national and European level – did not continue to inhibit us almost daily in the use of digitalisation, then we Germans with our engineers and entrepreneurs could once again take a leading position in progress following the examples of Krupp and Thyssen.

To keep up with this development meaningfully, however gradual it may be, we need entrepreneurial spirits like Robin Kiera. It is, therefore, rewarding to have been part of his entrepreneurial development, and I look forward to continuing this productive collaboration.

Dr Stefan Knoll
CEO of Deutsche Familienversicherung
May 2021

Introduction

Why do people camp out for several nights outside Apple Stores for the chance to buy an iPhone or other new gadget? How does Tesla sell its cars when the company does not advertise and does not have any conventional car dealerships? You may know the answer: customers flock to those products because Apple and Tesla have managed to generate 'hype' around the products they sell. There is hardly a need for a sales campaign – and seemingly no pressure for those companies when entering the market with a new product.

What a difference this is compared to most companies and industries! In fact, it is almost ridiculous that people will queue up to buy fancy mobile phones and luxury products yet products that promote and protect a family's health, like insurance, have to be pushed heavy-handedly into the market. Insurers and agents like us help people in their darkest hours, so people should be queuing up for our products, right?

Unfortunately, they are not – despite the billions invested in sales and marketing. Something isn't working!

In my opinion, it's our own fault. Imagine an agent complaining about a lack of customers who then drives to the customer's old address rather than their new address. Or think of an insurer phoning an old phone number of an insured person – despite being aware of the changed number. That is to say, we are using outdated methods to interface with our customers. The arguments 'This has worked for years' or 'We have always done it this way' are unreasonable. Yet many in our industry still think this way.

Fundamentally, the problem is that we are not where the customer is. The industry is spending billions frantically clinging to outdated communication strategies and content formats and channels, despite the fact that the customer is clearly no longer to be found there.

My company, Digitalscouting, is a marketing agency and consulting company, and its mission is to enable insurers, banks, and all companies with complex products and potentially physical sales forces to use the newest digital strategies, tactics, and hacks. We are here to support the good, the brave, and the rebels in these industries. And that's what this book is all about.

Let me ask you some hard questions about our industry:

- Why do insurance companies spend vast sums of money on TV advertising even though viewers check their mobile phones during the commercials?

- Why do agents call their customers on the phone when the customer is not interested and then wonder why they are not selling new products?
- Why do we invest in new communication, marketing, and sales channels when it is far too late?
- Why do we resist new trends and technologies instead of using them to our advantage?

The answers to these questions are often that it has 'always been this way'. But you'll come to realise that this is not a valid argument after reading this book.

This book is divided into two parts. The chapters in Part I cover some of the problems of the industry and what attention hacking is, and the chapters in Part II lay out the 10 practical steps, strategies, tactics, and tools that will help you sell insurance as successfully as Apple sells iPhones.

This book was written for entrepreneurs, marketers, intermediaries, and insurers seeking to invigorate their sales and marketing strategies. It is especially tailored for those in industries who struggle to attract customer interest, despite offering essential products and services. The book will also appeal to individuals seeking to understand the secrets behind the success of industry giants like Apple and how to apply these strategies to their own businesses.

Upon finishing the book, you will understand why conventional strategies fail to engage today's customers, who are largely found on digital and social media platforms. You'll learn how *attention hacking* can be employed to effectively capture and retain customer attention, leading to increased sales. You will gain insights from my personal journey of becoming a successful industry influencer and will be equipped with practical strategies to navigate the 'social media jungle'. The book underscores the importance of evolving with changing customer habits and needs and emphasises the power of innovation in dominating the marketplace.

Part I

Introducing Attention Hacking

In this part, I'll talk about the problems facing the insurance industry and what attention hacking is all about.

Chapter 1

Leading You Through the Digital Jungle Like Crocodile Dundee

Ln this chapter, you will learn:

- What's going wrong in the insurance industry
- Why we should talk plainly about what's going wrong
- That you can easily change course
- Strategies that will help you be successful in the future
- That attention is an important currency
- How this book will assist you

Are your customers interested in whether insurance comes from Allianz, Amazon, or a large comparison site? Usually not, because they decide to purchase insurance based on personal preferences such as cost, convenience, and urgency. Although there has not yet been a disruptive Uber-like moment in most insurance industries, the current dominance of your traditional insurance company is not assured. Think of Kodak, Polaroid, or Toys 'R' Us. They were once dominant in their industries, too. Then, at some point, digital cameras and online shopping became easier and cooler than a heavy analogue camera or driving to a shop. However, I don't want the insurance industry to suffer the same fate as the German mail-order companies, especially as there are good strategies available to prevent this fate.

If you're old enough, think back to the blockbuster movie *Crocodile Dundee: A Crocodile to Kiss* from 1986 – a comedy where the hero (named Crocodile Dundee) uses unconventional and rugged yet charming methods to survive in the wilderness. (If you haven't seen it, go check it out on a streaming service since we'll use it as a metaphor here!) Now ask yourself the following question: Would you want to have Crocodile Dundee or a qualified zookeeper as a partner if you were released into the wild?

Although Dundee would probably not fit in at a board of directors' dinner with his rugged manner, he is more likely to ensure your survival in the wild than the zookeeper. Nothing against zookeepers! They may have observed wild animals at close range, but Crocodile Dundee has evaded hungry crocodiles and starvation umpteen times. Because of his experience, he knows every trick in the book, and he will find a way through the jungle with you.

Consider this book as a survival guide for the digital jungle. It contains insights from dozens of campaigns with thousands of posts, videos, graphics, and millions of views. However, I apologise in advance, where, figuratively speaking, I bring out a machete to cut through the dense jungle undergrowth – meaning the traditional ways to market insurance.

Why Me and Why This Book?

Why should you trust me and read this book? Currently, I run Digitalscouting, serving clients in Europe and Asia, which, in German-speaking countries, is one of the best-known marketing agencies and consulting companies in the insurance industry. It has offices in Germany and the Philippines and employs about 30 people. The company has supported breathtaking turn-around cases and run some of the most successful and radical campaigns. It has transformed sales managers into influencers and acts as external marketing and social media departments in a large number of cases. Part of the offering is to run LinkedIn accounts for business leaders and C-suites and some of the biggest TikTok, Instagram, and YouTube channels of the industry. Alternatively, we help to push transformation in large corporations. We also design and produce some of the hottest and most modern advertising campaigns in central Europe.

How does Digitalscouting do this? Apart from a ninja team, we really understand the industry. I started my career in the insurance industry as an insurance sales agent. And you know what? I would not miss that time for all the money in the world. Why? Because I really know how it feels to try to sell a policy to a hard-working family, and I know the critical questions customers have. I also understand how agents and brokers think. As a result, my company can deliver strategies and content that really work.

After my time as a sales manager, a project manager in operations, and a manager in a start-up, I worked as chief product officer at the digital subsidiary of Hamburg-based private bank M. M. Warburg & Co. I also learned about many new trends, technologies, and apps during extended stays in the United States and China. The changes in communication and customers' buying behaviour over the past two decades have become apparent to me. At the same time, I saw virtually no movement in the insurance and finance industry with how agents approached customers. They continued to cold call customers when it was obvious that wasn't working. I saw interviews with board members who pretended, and in some cases still pretend, that the annoying Internet will soon disappear and that people's communication and buying behaviour will remain the same. (I still do not understand this complete misreading of the situation!)

Thankfully, I didn't have to take corporate considerations into account. However, at the same time, I was able to point to two apps that had earned over US$1 billion in cash and had connected a billion assets under information. I used this knowledge to begin to explain the situation in the insurance industry in a less diplomatic, but entertaining, way. At the same time, I started Digitalscouting.de as a light-hearted blog and took my first steps on social media. The response was huge. In early 2017, Moritz Finkelnburg described me in a blog post as a relevant Insurtech influencer – it took me a moment to look up what he meant by that. After that, the number of followers I had on LinkedIn, Twitter, YouTube, and Xing increased steadily. Today I have more than 600,000 followers, and I get between 10 and 20 million views per month.

My plain language had an unforeseen side effect. Some of the most controversial keynote speeches generated, on the one hand, furious responses and, on the other, inquiries from the insurance industry. Many managers wanted to talk to me about strategy, marketing, and sales. From the first orders, Digitalscouting developed as a marketing agency and consulting firm. I left my job as chief product officer with a heavy heart to continue building Digitalscouting. And it paid off! Today, around 30 experts work for us, and we have been able to implement some of the best-known campaigns and strategy projects both in Germany and internationally.

These and the general developments internationally did not go unnoticed by many corporate headquarters and individuals. The industry is slowly starting to rethink its approach. However, many people in charge still opt for established channels and formats. This happens either out of ignorance or so as not to be vulnerable within a group by taking risks. After all, everyone else is using those same established strategies. This may keep you safe professionally in the short term, but it does not gain you any new business, and eventually it will lose you business.

In addition to the outdated strategies, we also have to ignore the established standards of the marketing agency circus. A whole ecosystem of conferences and competitions exists around established, often outdated and over-priced, channels and formats. This celebrates itself and only revolves around itself. But we don't want prizes. We want to survive in the wild like Crocodile Dundee, as well as win customers and sales! For our customers. For you.

Solution
Win customers, not prizes!

Four Themes Throughout This Book

In this book, I show you ways to safely navigate the digital wilderness, adapting and turning former threats into opportunities. These are the four central points you'll find when reading the following pages:

- The takeaways from this book are not rocket science. Instead, they allow you to learn from others and avoid making expensive mistakes – no matter where your company is located, whether you work as an agent, in the company or as staff.
- You can learn from the practical examples in this book, including the good and the bad.
- You need to radically rethink things! You will survive only if you adapt your marketing and sales to the rapidly changing environment that is the digital world today. Moreover, if you do it really well, you will experience exponential growth.
- It just takes 10 easy steps to immediately start selling insurance like it's an iPhone.

Read This Book in Four Days or Less

You will learn strategies that will make you and your company embody the solution to a problem your customers are facing – strategies that are easy to apply and do not require spending millions needlessly. For example, we at Digitalscouting know what content, formats, and channels are important, how often we need to post and when a campaign is more suitable for YouTube or TikTok. Over the past 10 years we have established several well-known influencers for our customers, and we are now considered to be one of the leading influencers in the international insurance industry. How we got there is not a secret. On the remaining pages, I will explain it step by step. You will reach your goal if you set concrete milestones!

The value of the book is not in its retail price but in the additional customers and sales you can generate for yourself or your brokerage by applying the content. However, there is still one hurdle in your way. You actually have to make a start. You can only achieve success if you take action – and to do that you need deadlines. So work through this book in four days or less. Reread it in three months' time. Don't think of these pages as another reference book for the bookcase, but as a survival guide for the digital world and a starting point for above-average growth.

Trust Is Key

In 2009, I found a TV on Amazon and agonised for days over whether I should make the €700 purchase. Even though I had been used to buying books and small goods from Amazon for years, my concern was that I would be stuck with my defective device if I had any issues with it because there was no third-party address or direct contact to deal with. It was a large purchase, and I didn't quite trust Amazon yet. When I finally purchased the TV, the delivery went smoothly. However, it didn't take long for the TV to break – and Amazon organised a repair for me without any problems!

In one fell swoop, my shopping behaviour changed completely. Since then, I have trusted Amazon and even purchased expensive items online. The ordering process is too smooth, the selection too tempting. Now I order almost everything for my home and Digitalscouting via Amazon. Amazon's investment of US$100 for the smooth repair of a US$600 TV turned into a US$100,000+ client. Well done, Jeff Bezos!

Amazon's success reinforces the lesson that trust is the basic condition for purchases, and this is especially true in insurance sales. After all, there are more important things at stake in insurance sales than a TV (which still works, by the way)!

Everything Is Changing All the Time

Society and the economy – our entire world order – are undergoing radical changes at an unprecedented pace. Video cassettes once dominated the market for decades, but then CDs, DVDs, and Blu-ray discs came on the scene. But they were subsequently replaced for the most part by streaming services.

The life span of products in the digital world is becoming increasingly shorter. The same is true for the Internet. It took decades from the first email ever sent in 1971 for there to be widespread change in buying and communication behaviour. However, mobile phones, mobile Internet, social networks, and social influence are changing people's behaviours today at lightning speeds.

The insurance industry considers itself to be in the middle between traditional industries and cutting-edge ones, but it must pick up the pace to keep up. People today have different expectations of products and communication. If we ignore the digital revolution, customers will buy their insurance in the future from comparison sites such as Google and Amazon – or one of the innovative reinsurers or primary insurers. Whether you like it or not, our industry is under a lot of pressure to keep up!

Despite massive opportunities, efficiency gains, and new risks, most insurance industries are barely growing, with the exception of a few fields and positive examples. That's a pity, because growth should be possible. If you want to change this, you have to be able to reach new and existing customers in a better way. We have to be where the customers are, especially on social networks. Therefore, we should consistently rely on YouTube, Twitter, LinkedIn, TikTok, and the like, when selling insurance. From my own experience, I can assure you that this strategy works. We have gained new customers for our clients and my own company by building and using social media influencers.

Social media influencers are people who use their presence and high profile on social networks to spread opinions or promote products and lifestyles, for example. The prerequisites for an influencer's success are social authority, trustworthiness, and consistent behaviour – all this helps them to attract the attention of their audience.

This is precisely what our concept of attention hacking, with the help of influencers, is all about. It permanently places insurers and agents on the customer's radar. Then they won't contact their main bank when the need arises, but us instead. It is not that difficult to bring about this change. This book shows you what you need to do to achieve this.

Attention Hacking: Getting on the Customer's Radar

Attention hacking – what this book is all about – refers to the strategic approach of consistently positioning your brand or service in the consumer's everyday life by providing relevant and valuable content in up-to-date formats across their preferred channels. The aim is to establish trust, gain influence, and ultimately become the go-to solution for a specific problem the customer faces, thus transforming their attention into business success. This is not a mere marketing tactic but a mindset aiming for exceptional growth and success.

Let's go back in time. When I was supposed to generate 'points and pieces' (selling insurance policies) as an insurance broker, we were handed randomly compiled telephone lists every month. During many phone calls, I heard similar things over and over again: 'Nice of you to call. Four months ago we bought a house. Our main bank helped us with the financing and the insurance.' In the moment of need, the customer did not think of me as an agent or the insurance group worth billions in the background. In traditional insurance distribution, an enormous amount of business is lost because the customer does not think of us as a solution to their problems in the moment of need.

Getting on the customers' radar is vital for survival. Having good sales and profit figures right now will not protect you. Kodak, Polaroid, and Toys 'R' Us had good, years, too – before they all collapsed. Do not rely on seemingly positive business figures! It is certain that technology companies such as Amazon and Apple will also emerge in the insurance industry. We just don't know the names of these disruptors yet. It doesn't necessarily have to be new players. Some traditional competitors – insurers and reinsurers – are still working semi-covertly, but diligently, on their modernisation. They are already using attention-hacking strategies. You should not be afraid of these new challenges either! There are tried and tested strategies that you can use to retain existing customers and partners and attract new ones.

> ## Solution
> Always be on the customer's radar.

This book is not just about social media. It is about a much broader basic principle. If you want to be at the forefront of customers' minds in the moment of need, you have to establish yourself in their everyday lives. This is achieved at great expense by constantly booking all available advertising channels. However, there is a more efficient way to do this. Just occupy the space where the customer's attention is and where your competitors are not yet.

The strategy is simple: deliver the following to your target group:

- Relevant content that they actually consume
- On the channels they currently use
- In the formats that correspond to their real consumption preferences
- In the frequency the communities and algorithms demand
- At the quality the channels want

Instead, many rely on traditional channels and formats, such as television and radio commercials and print advertisements in newspapers, magazines, and brochures, that have long since lost people's attention. They are like a hunter aiming at the spot where the deer grazed yesterday. Do better! Internalise the ethos of a true hunter. Keep the customer in your sights at all times.

Then, go where the attention is! Put yourself forward as a trusted partner, offer ongoing help, and stay on the radar. Give people a reason to work with you. Burn yourself into your customers' consciousness, so there is no way to bypass you. You don't have to sell proactively; people will come to you. Nevertheless of course, it's still a good idea to sell actively.

Be where the customers actually are. Yesterday, they sat in front of CNN and BBC, today they use social media, and tomorrow it could be something completely different. Remember the basic principle outlined: You have to establish yourself or your company in the day-to-day world of your target group. Position yourself there as a solution provider for a specific problem and transform people's attention into business success. This idea can be described as follows:

1. Listen. Go where your customers are – whether digital or analogue.
2. Make yourself visible with valuable and helpful content in formats that your target group actually consumes. Avoid clumsy advertising and explanations of products.
3. This content generates attention and builds trust.
4. Trust helps you gain influence and, as a result, influencer status.
5. People turn to you the moment a problem crops up and when you are seen as the solution to that problem or they are more open when you contact them directly.
6. When this happens, you have generated a pull out of the market from a push into the market.
7. The result: Attention helps you to get new customers and to sell more to existing clients!

This principle works only if you share relevant content in modern and up-to-date formats. So, forget the old advertising and marketing tactics. Stop trying to please customers or stick to channels that no longer work by force or based on some monthly calling lists. Numerous insurers still have traditional advertising films produced for hundreds of thousands of

US dollars, which nobody watches apart from the board of directors and the supervisory board, and which then fade away on YouTube with 300 views or have to be pumped out on TV to the tune of millions. Even there, no one is paying attention anymore. People switch the TV to mute when they see an advert, they use their mobile phone, go to the kitchen or the bathroom. The impact gained from the millions spent is next to zero. There are, however, far more efficient methods to get people's attention. Attention hacking allows you, as a company and as an agent, to become part of people's lives. You become a trusted partner – or a (micro)influencer, if we want to use the latest terminology. That is why attention hacking is not a technology or a marketing approach. Instead, it is a new mindset that aims for above-average success and growth.

The value of each influencer is measured in categories such as quality and quantity of reach, attention, and effectiveness. This way, their advice and opinions carry weight. If you only transmit information and ignore the customer's needs, you will never become an influencer or you have already been one for a very long time. What is worse is when companies do not respond to comments or they completely turn off the comment function. Such practices reduce social media to absurdity and demonstrate a total lack of interest in the customer. They can even damage a brand.

Toolbox: Wefox vs Lemonade

Influencers can even solve real problems. In 2018, two of the biggest and most renowned Insurtechs were heading for a legal battle – and Lemonade's lawsuit against Wefox could have caused considerable damage to the

(continued)

(*continued*)

emerging Insurtech movement. As a result of my network and presence in the insurance community, I knew both CEOs. I was in contact with both of them via Whats App and let Lemonade boss Daniel know that I thought his actions were regrettable – and I also did so publicly as an influencer in a critical article. It goes without saying I told him about it beforehand.

I was also in contact with Julian Teicke, co-founder and CEO of Wefox, at the same time. I knew and respected both of them. They just didn't have a direct line to each other. Based on the trust built up over the years, I brought them together on one condition: no lawyers in the room, just the three of us.

In a 10-hour marathon session, we were able to clear up all the contentious issues and prevent an escalation. It was only because I personally know and respect Julian and Daniel that I knew both were exceptional entrepreneurial individuals and that direct contact between them could work.

Networking and building trust pays off – for everyone involved! It saved both parties and the community a lot of time and hassle. Attention hacking also works in this respect.

Solution
Become an influencer.

Chapter 2

'It's the Mindset, Stupid.'*

In this chapter, you will learn:

- Why we previously completely overlooked existential risks
- That you must never lose sight of the core objective to achieve growth
- Why you should follow the example of Apple, Google, and others
- That everything will change
- Why people should be thinking about us all the time
- Why you should forget the term *normal*

During a discussion about expanding the value chain, a realisation hit me like a bolt of lightning: most insurers

*Adapted from Bill Clinton. With the help of constant reminders of the principle 'It's the economy, stupid!' Bill Clinton won the US presidential election in 1992. His primary focus was on the economic prosperity of Americans.

and agents sell only one product, insurance. It is rare for other business areas to generate significant revenues and profits in the insurance industry. Ironically, the industry that is so excellent at assessing risk is itself so risky! Relying on one product category is always risky, but especially so in an uncertain socio-political environment. Therefore, deepening the value chain and expanding it are both means for growth, as well as necessary to protect a company's core.

Nevertheless, many insurers continue to rely on the perceived cash cow of selling insurance since it has been doing well for a considerable time.

Meanwhile, there is a lack of thinking outside the box regarding innovations in the industry. One of the reasons why we don't notice the threat of being left behind is because of an endless career merry-go-round. We prefer to steal each other's decision-makers instead of getting fresh, external input. Why not make the head of development at Google the chief technology officer (CTO) of your company or the Insurtech founder the head of strategy? That could lead to innovation instead of hiring from within the industry.

Instead, many insurers focus almost exclusively on the development of even more sophisticated insurance terms and conditions, more sophisticated risk calculations, or more and more psychologised sales methods. This narrow approach turns a blind eye to social change and the new challenges of digitalisation. Yet, like all businesses, insurers thrive on risk minimisation and growth. Anyone who stands in the way of these goals will be punished by losing business, sooner or later.

From Strollers to a New Business Model

This is the key question facing all businesses:

How do we manage to grow as fast, as sustainably, and as safely as possible?

This question is difficult to answer for the insurance industry. An underlying problem is that we have been successful for so long. Therefore, we believe as insurers that we cannot do certain things. However, insurance is not so special that it has to follow certain rules. An insurer is – economically speaking – nothing but the accumulation of capital on a mission to turn capital into more capital on the basis of its activity. If we accept this idea, it liberates us from our self-imposed shackles. Why shouldn't we recommend strollers or sell clothing?

Before the critics start throwing regulations into the mix, all it takes is a handful of proactive lawyers to develop a clever structure for non-insurance benefits. We cannot count on regulators to defend apathy and inaction – it's not their job – particularly seeing that the supervisory authority has a keen interest in solid and stable insurers.

Let's get back to talking about strollers. Years ago, the manager of a large brokerage became a father at the same time as I did. While discussing our newborn babies, the conversation turned to work and specifically attention hacking. His theory was that an agent could not engage in attention hacking under any circumstances and should stick with the traditional methods of reaching customers. We argued a bit, but in the end, I asked him how he found the best stroller for his new baby.

He answered like everyone else: 'I asked friends, family, and Google.' I quickly replied, 'Why not your insurer?' While he initially reacted in amazement, he quickly agreed that insurers have a lot of valuable insight into their customers' everyday issues. For example, they know the best stroller when it comes to accidents or health insurance.

The new father and brokerage manager came to the same conclusion that I've been getting at in this section. 'Then we could also recommend or sell strollers,' he said. That would not only be attention hacking, but also expanding the business model into new products.

Identify Drivers of Growth

It is always important to identify drivers of growth and use them consistently. From my point of view, we achieve this goal when the insurance industry builds a better relationship with its customers and offers them the opportunity to spend even more of their budget with us. Only when people perceive us and trust us as a solution provider will they buy our insurance and other products. The strategic goal of every insurer – and all other companies as well – is therefore quite simple: to dominate their customers' attention.

The best-in-class for identifying drivers of growth is Red Bull. For me, Red Bull is great at marketing. Even early on they did not rely on distribution via traditional media only but invented sports events with the sole purpose of generating content and a community for their brand. Examples include Red Bull Flugtag, a competition of homemade, human-powered flying machines, and Red Bull Stratos, a high-altitude diving project.

When social media was invented, Red Bull created breath-taking content from popular and fun sport events. It was also a smart move by them to take over a small soccer club near Leipzig and make it into R(ed) B(ull) Leipzig, investing wisely and pushing the club into the Bundesliga and Champions League. This was a cheap way to get the attention that others need to spend millions doing by advertising via TV commercials during halftime.

Red Bull is just one example. Google, Facebook, and Amazon also dominate attention in the marketplace. Consumers use Google to search for whatever they need, stay in touch on Facebook, and buy suitable products on Amazon without giving a thought to using a different company.

When it comes to topics such as security, risk provision, or money, the obvious instinct should be to visit Allianz, MetLife, Allstate, Achmea, Aegon, Baloise, Helvetia, and Wiener Städtische. Insurance companies need to be the first choice for customers when they think about insurance, just like Google is for Internet searches. The success of companies like Google, Facebook, and Amazon show that being top-of-mind for customers is a key factor for business growth. By applying the same principle, insurance companies can grow their business by becoming the go-to choice for their customers' insurance needs, instead of letting these market behemoths take over. So, let's aim for dominance at least within our niche, with our target group and with our products. In the context of our issues, Silicon Valley corporations should play a subordinate role in the insurance industry at the most.

Set Unrealistic Goals

While completely reinventing shopping, communication, and mobility seem like lofty goals, that's exactly what people like Jeff Bezos, Mark Zuckerberg, and Elon Musk did when launching Amazon, Facebook, and Tesla, respectively. These leaders believed in themselves and their visions and gave it their all to realise them. We can do that, too! Admittedly, these are very ambitious footsteps to follow, but why not?

The goal, in the context of the insurance industry, is to revolutionise the sector by creating innovative and customer-focused products and services, leveraging technology for efficiency, and offering an exceptional customer experience. This could redefine how people perceive and interact with insurance, making it more accessible, intuitive, and beneficial for them. So, let's not just reimagine insurance, let's revolutionise it.

The Radical Transformation of OCC Assekuradeur

When Désirée Mettraux took over as the new managing director at insurance provider OCC Assekuradeur, nothing externally gave away the market leader's precarious situation. IT integration was paralysing the company, service problems were leaving customers and agents in a state of despair, and there was very little in the way of digital processes. Furthermore, the historically ingrained structures made it challenging to solve problems and generate more significant growth.

Mettraux set herself the unrealistic goal of radically transforming OCC within 12 months and making it fit for the future. This included the complete replacement of middle management, reversal of IT integration, modernisation of the brand, a relaunch of marketing, a culture change, the introduction of attention hacking, repositioning of sales, and expansion of the business model.

One summer morning I urged Désirée to start a presence on TikTok for OCC. So the company did. We made it the leading insurance channel on TikTok, and even though she eventually left the company and Marcel Neumann became one of her successors, we reached millions and millions of people in the core target group. Furthermore, we expanded the TikTok strategy to a short-video strategy additionally distributed on Instagram and YouTube, which reached millions more customers. If we had wanted to reach the same number of people with ads in car magazines, we would have had to spend more than US$20 million. Needless to say, our social media budget was significantly smaller.

Although the transformation is far from complete, OCC now processes more than 65% of all applications automatically (compared to 0%!). OCC has established itself as a modern brand on social media and is increasingly recognised as demonstrating best practices in radically modernising a successful, outdated niche insurer at lightning speed.

Mettraux and her team managed to win over experts and industry experts from outside the sector during the transformation. They also retained long-serving specialists internally and mobilised them for modernisation. Doing so enabled them to bring together a powerful team. This team was so strong that the success continued long after she left the company.

All of Mettraux's goals in the beginning seemed completely unattainable. But unrealistic goals are at the core of attention hacking. It's about thinking the unthinkable and achieving the unachievable.

You Want New Problems

Breaking industry boundaries means being liberated from decades-old shackles. However, this breakthrough is not always subject to entertainment tax. In other words, the process of breaking industry boundaries and innovating isn't always fun or entertaining. There may be criticism, unexpected challenges, and stressful situations. However, these difficulties are signs of progress and should be welcomed as they lead to new opportunities and skill acquisition.

When carving out new paths, you will also encounter new challenges. IT systems will buckle under the weight of customers, service providers will fall to their knees, and all sorts of drama will take you by surprise. Even the best analysis and strategy and the most daring modernisation do not lead to the peace of mind that many large organisations would like.

Yet new problems are exactly what you want. They mean that you have reached a new level, where new opportunities will arise and new levels of success are possible. By solving new problems, you will also continue to acquire new skills.

Him Again!

When I started Digitalscouting, I was often ridiculed for posting selfies and stories on social media from conferences and trips all over the world. A conference attendee once commented on my recordings in Frankfurt by saying, 'Now I also know that you came by train.' The comment was a slight dig, but I thought to myself, 'Yes, but so did 20,000 other people.'

When you are breaking new ground, you have to accept a little ridicule sometimes. A little while later decision-makers and experts from the insurance industry and banking started contacting me to meet for coffee. I was in so much demand that that's when I decided to start my own management consultancy and marketing company. If I had listened to my colleague in Frankfurt and sheepishly packed up my camera and stopped taking and posting selfies, Digitalscouting would never have happened.

Fun fact: years later the aforementioned colleague contacted me and also became a client of Digitalscouting.

Fight Normalcy

In this world that we live in, there is no 'normal' and no state of rest. Problems arise in both decline and recovery. Due to the accelerated increase in the complexity of the world, there can be no standstill and no normal state. Once Nokia phones, 0% interest, and mail-order catalogues were standard. But none of these are available today. No sooner do the general conditions change that a business model can begin to unravel. It's tough to answer the following questions in a constantly changing world: What should a typical budget be? What should define a typical year?

In insurance, standing still and accepting the status quo are expressions of giving up. Instead, you should see normality, standing still, and your comfort zone as your greatest opponents. The industry should challenge traditional methods, create new insurance products, and embrace digital transformation. Change is now the new reality due to digital disruption, changing customer expectations, and shifting risk landscapes. Companies that learn from trends and improve their skills survive and grow, turning change into opportunities for a competitive edge.

Create something new! Continuously embracing change and learning to deal with new tools, tactics, and trends is not a one-off reaction, but a crucial skill. Those who consciously develop this ability can repeatedly take on new challenges. Not only will they survive, but they will use the change as a great opportunity.

In the insurance sector, pseudo-stability, or ignoring the signs of change, is a costly, shortsighted approach. Companies may convince themselves that industry disruptions won't affect them, using significant resources to maintain status quo and repel external influences. This leads to a culture resistant to innovation and fresh ideas, undermining growth and adaptability and ultimately threatening the business's viability in the evolving market. This tactic also consumes an enormous number of resources. In this way, people waste expertise and capacity to justify the status quo argument and to fend off external input. This creates a corporate culture where every suggestion is shot down.

Unfortunately, the entrenched hierarchies and an error-intolerant corporate culture often punish those who dare to put their head above the parapet like the Bezos, Zuckermans, and Musks of the world. But successfully engaging employees' minds requires action!

Data Protection vs Lunch

When I worked as an executive at one of the larger insurers, the people in charge wanted to promote interaction between the strongly divided silos of the company. So, to set a good example, I created an inter-departmental and cross-hierarchical WhatsApp group so that everyone could arrange to meet for lunch via the text messaging app.

A division manager, who was also younger, reported enthusiastically, in an official committee, about this attempt to dissolve the silos. Shortly thereafter, I learned that sharing details like this between colleagues was not allowed due to 'data protection reasons', even though it was a private group. The sacred silos were being protected with an excuse of data protection.

Hey, don't show any initiative – you might get new ideas. To avoid further compromising myself politically, I closed the WhatsApp group. That evening I spoke with some headhunters on the phone, and a few weeks later, I left the regional insurer as a result of this and other experiences of the company not being open to innovation.

Chapter 3
Sales Is Broken, and Operations Has Seen Better Times

In this chapter, you will learn:

- That the corporate culture in the insurance industry is often toxic
- How, despite great products, it has a negative public image
- Why existing goals are leading us to ruin
- That there are still many great people in the insurance industry
- The fatal effect that some internal structures can have

The current state of the insurance industry could be better. We need a fresh outlook and new tools to keep up in today's economy. Most companies are using legacy IT and outdated sales and marketing concepts. Most companies in the industry have a disastrous mindset and the culture in insurance companies can be toxic. It's a dismal outlook, but that's why you're reading this book.

Need for a Fresh Outlook

I learned that lesson myself. That's how I started my career in the medical technology sector at B. Braun Melsungen AG. The company was shaped by the incredible fairness, reliability, and friendliness of the then CEO and owner Ludwig Georg Braun. It was a matter of course for him to be true to his word. On the periphery of a reception, he made a promise to me, and years later, he kept it. The list of similar anecdotes about him could fill books. This reliability and sincerity could be felt in all parts of the company I became acquainted with at that time.

Now, in my decades-long career in insurance, I have come across plenty of incredibly nice, honest, and committed employees in sales and operations. I remember the countless agents and employees who positively assisted customers and colleagues. Excellent agents always wanted to achieve what was best for their company as well as what made sense for the customer.

However, I have also repeatedly witnessed – mostly outside my organisation – questionable treatment of clients and colleagues.

- Line managers shouting at salespeople
- Promises and assurances made the day before counting for nothing count
- Instead of advising customers according to their needs, managers forcibly pushing a certain product onto the market

This was the case not only with the usual suspects but also sometimes with reputable agents.

So, I am not surprised that many agents' Internet ratings as employers are abysmal, aside from a few glowing reports. The turnover rate is also alarming. A sales director I know recently reported the following: out of about 25 new, young sales managers in a cohort, about 50% had left after 6 months and about 75% after 1 year. This senseless waste of money spent on training new hires only to have them leave and take that training elsewhere urgently needs to be examined. Many companies already have problems recruiting young people – the pull of new insurance companies with low entry barriers is too great. Although the pay in the new companies is also relatively low, they offer a positive corporate culture and future opportunities.

Elisabeth Stiller, head of sales at the General Association of the German Insurance Industry, recently noted that the number of insurance agents has been decreasing for years. Why is this?

The reasons for the decline in the number of agents registered are manifold. One important point is that in recent years, throughout Europe, there are stricter requirements for entering and practising the profession. You can't become an insurance agent 'just like that' anymore.

Of course, demographic trends also have an impact. About 40% of registered insurance agents are 55 years of age and older. You are dealing with company succession, at least in terms of perspective, at a time when distribution is in a state of upheaval. Good young talent – communicative and empathetic, technically and digitally savvy – is in demand in many sectors.

Incidentally, this is exactly why we came up with our initiative Become an #Insurancer. We want to inspire young people with the right skills and attitude to enter insurance sales.

Trends Among Agents

The social distancing that happened as a result of the COVID-19 pandemic, on one hand, was an enormous entrepreneurial challenge for agents and, on the other hand, a boost for digitalisation in sales. As an association of insurance companies, we are not in direct contact with the agents. That being said, I noticed that many agent companies adapted quickly and flexibly to the new circumstances. The job is not just limited to professional expertise and the ability to sell. Skills such as entrepreneurship, flexibility, perspective, and a willingness to continuously learn are also part of it. The fact that the industry has come through the recent COVID-19 pandemic unscathed is also largely thanks to the agents.

What do successful agents do differently today, and what do agents have to do to continue to be successful in the future? To be successful, they have to make their business fit for the future and keep it in good shape. To do this, they need to be able to anticipate change. This applies both to the behaviour and expectations of their customers and to trends among the providers they cooperate with. They have to keep an eye on the competition, including potential competitors. This is challenging and exciting. Young people want to join companies that offer prospects.

No One Wants (or Is Able) to Sell Insurance Any Longer

Insurance sales today still often mean calling people from customer lists on the phone, making appointments, and advising customers in their living rooms or over video. One problem with this is that cold-calling people are perceived as a nuisance – even if you have a great product.

Moreover, this effort is simply no longer worthwhile for many products, such as liability or household contents, not least due to the extensive agency documentation required. One consequence of this trend is the decrease in the number of agents.[1] In 2018, it was particularly dire, with more than 20,000 agents having to or wanting to quit. Many smaller companies in particular are now operating unprofitably.

Despite agents' essential role at an insurance company and regardless of their expertise in financial and asset matters, the work of a consultant and seller is not valued by customers or companies, which is unfortunate. Although many insurers claim customer satisfaction as their slogan, these factors do not play a major role when it comes to commissions for employees and recognising sales success. Instead, only sales seem to count. This certainly has consequences for the distribution channels. Who has not experienced colleagues being celebrated on stage at kick-off or end-of-year events when everyone knew they had not always made the customer's interests the focus of their efforts? It is the open, honest, and committed agents – of which there are many thousands – as well as the good insurers who suffer from this type of environment.

[1] www.handelsblatt.com/finanzen/banken-versicherungen/vermittler-professoren-erwarten-grossesvermittlersterben/8968118-3.html?ticket=ST-808890-1VJfLXQwpqWaIxC1bayi-ap1www.procontra-online.de/artikel/date/2018/10/knapp-2000-weniger-vermittlersterben-haelt-an

No New Clients

A client of Digitalscouting improved their market presence through attention hacking, leading to faster establishment of business-to-business (B2B) partnerships. This client, a B2B company, no longer needed to spend time explaining their business to potential partners due to their increased visibility. This led to quickly formed sales partnerships. However, this surge in business strained their IT department, a problem indicative of their success.

Potential partners noticed the difference in approach, and a great sales partnership was quickly established. One problem that resulted was that IT was not able to process the high volume of new customers. Needless to say, that was a good problem to have.

Illogical Sales Targets

'The fish stinks from the head' is a saying in northern Germany. This means that if there's a problem in a group or company, it's usually caused by the people at the top, such as the leaders or bosses.

This also applies to insurers. The catalyst for many troublesome trends is short-term and rigid turnover or sales targets. Unfortunately, they are often at odds with longer-term success and lead to setting the wrong strategic course. For example, someone who wants to build the best sales division in Germany in 10 years' time has to act very differently today than someone who wants to close as many deals as possible this year. In a digital world, rigid goals backfire.

It is also downright bizarre that sales targets often look the same for everyone – even though the target groups, client portfolios, and framework conditions of the individual agents vary greatly. On top of that, there is a huge discrepancy between training and reality. Academic content is taught on the job that has little if anything to do with actual sales – often by people who can't really demonstrate any practical success.

End of Operations as We Know It

Everyone is familiar with those companies whose office buildings exude the dilapidated charm of the 1970s for ordinary employees. The board of directors, on the other hand, rush to a separate, well-designed floor at the top in a separate elevator, with assistants in tailored suits and liveried servants. Don't get me wrong, I don't begrudge anyone this sort of luxury. But those who move exclusively in such a sealed-off world often lose touch with reality.

Toolbox: The Coloured Button

During a strategy meeting of a large German regional insurer, 15 experts were discussing the development of a new app. I was freshly poached from a gaming start-up to take over 'under-board' responsibility for parts of this modernisation.

When the IT director responsible for the project entered the room, the entire room fell silent. Instead of offering feedback on substantial features or improvements, the director gave detailed instructions on minor matters of the app development such as elements of the

(continued)

(*continued*)

user interface. That's why, 14 days later, the developers presented the app's freshly coloured buttons as the sum of their work over the past 2 weeks.

These were trivial changes that should not have taken 2 weeks. The fact that the IT director, and the board, praised these minor changes indicated they lacked understanding of the technical aspects of the project. This misunderstanding allowed the development team to make minimal progress while giving the impression they were working hard.

This type of scenario was repeated numerous times on the project. I asked the boss privately what he really thought of the team's work progress. 'It's great', he replied. I understood then that his technical expertise as the IT director was so limited that he did not realise that an inexperienced intern could have made those types of changes during a lunch break.

In addition, the board did not even understand that the IT director lacked the expertise to make good decisions for his division that was creating the app. Even if the experts in the company shared my view, the toxic culture of the company meant that no one dared to tell the truth, certainly not in a meeting.

To date, this insurer worth billions is yet to have a marketable app. The damage to the company and the lost opportunities because of the company's culture were considerable.

When the board of directors is so out of touch with the details of a project, nothing will get done. By the way, no meetings or reports can help combat this detachment.

For example, one company I worked for used a traffic light rating system in their project reports, but it was meaningless because they always set all projects to green, despite any obstacles they were facing. I had the guts to change some of the evergreen traffic lights in project reporting to amber. The result was that the chief information officer (CIO) got enraged and demanded that the results be fudged as usual and everything switched back to green. He could not afford this loss of face in front of his board colleagues. Reality was hidden in order to save face, even though the projects were on fire. However, the right answers to the ever-present change can only be found by those who respect reality. Therefore, my advice to all the industry's detached decision-makers is to return to society's reality and that of your workforces! Get out of the boardroom. A machine that has become independent can hardly do anything to challenge the Amazons out there – despite all the green lights.

However, I would like to emphasise at the same time that many decision-makers who work in the insurance industry have a different background. As a result, we see veterans making the right decisions because they are realistic about the changes of today based on their experience. They have their feet on the ground and know the reality inside and outside the industry. They want the right outcome for customers and employees and behave accordingly. If such a manager reaches their individual limits, they bring in experts from outside. This does not make leaders weak, but rather it shows their strength.

Furthermore, we are seeing a new generation of board members and managing directors (of both genders) who are relentlessly modernising their organisations and, in so doing, trying to save them. These leaders give us hope.

Friendship Instead of Performance

It is actually nice to provide jobs to friends who have perhaps failed in other ventures. But if they lack the necessary qualifications, the company as a whole suffers.

This happens when old friends get divisional head jobs but no one knows exactly what they do all day. One of them got the executive role in a spin-off of the company. The first official act is to create new business cards with the wonderful new title. Pressing issues such as the business model, the business plan, recruiting, and product development can wait. Offices were rented without a plan and muddled decisions were made without consultation. It is no wonder that such leaders can't modernise.

The team didn't fare any better. When I went to the canteen after a workshop with the director, I wanted to say something supportive: 'It's nice that pensioners also have access to the canteen.' The director: 'That's our IT.' But if you haven't recruit anyone for almost 10 years, you can't be surprised about having an ageing workforce – especially in the technology sector. Such teams may struggle to compete against start-ups, tech companies, and competitors.

In conclusion, giving leadership roles to unqualified friends can harm a company. It also warns against neglecting recruitment, as an ageing workforce might struggle to compete with more dynamic and innovative competitors.

Chapter 4

Imagine It's the End-of-the-Year Selling Season and No One Is Listening

In this chapter, you will learn:

- How much communication behaviour and your customers have changed in the past decade
- How you should classify social media
- Why you first have to pay attention to the mobile accessibility of your offers
- Why you have to be present online and offline
- How to position yourself
- A shaky mobile phone picture is worth more than an expensive TV ad

People's communication behaviour has changed radically in recent years. The steady growth of social networks has led to the ongoing decline of established traditional media channels.

In the past, it was all about newspapers, radio, and TV. Today there are 10 billion mobile devices in the world, and more than 4.76 billion people worldwide used social media daily in 2023. In 2022 alone, 142 billion apps were downloaded. Was yours one of them?

As far as content goes, video is king. According to multiple sources, 65% of Internet traffic is video.

And guess what? Even as I write this, these numbers are out of date and increasing.

But it's not just that only media is so popular. It's popular with the right crowd. Today the average age of the viewers of German state TV is 62 years old when the average of the population is only 44. Why do insurers still advertise on outdated channels where their target group of young adults is in reality no longer represented?

Take a Hard Look at Social Media

Social media platforms provide a way to reach people directly, by way of attention hacking. In fact, social media is a godsend for our industry. It is about reaching people, exchanging ideas with them, and, in the end, winning them over so that they buy our products.

For a social media marketing strategy to work, keep these three goals in mind:

- You need to become part of people's everyday world.
- You need contact details to be able to contact people independently of agent social media channels and to direct them to your own ecosystem.

- People should approach you of their own accord when they need insurance.

You should include these three core objectives in any marketing and sales strategy. Expensive TV commercials can end up being useless. After all, TV commercials are no longer part of people's lives; they prefer to check WhatsApp during the commercial breaks. TV ads don't pull people in anymore. A strong focus on these three goals lays the foundation for a successful approach to (potential) customers.

New Business at Classic Car Insurer OCC Assekuradeur

Instead of focusing solely on classic and collector's car insurance, OCC Assekuradeur completely revamped the brand, expanded the target group beyond the core classic car community, and opened an online shop for lifestyle fashion, which is systematically advertised online.

While this shop is unlikely to replace the revenue of the insurance business, these experiments help a company to learn how to try new business models. Maybe later an idea will emerge from it that may very well have a significant impact on the balance sheet and therefore on the value of the company.

Mobile First

Because communication now mainly takes place via mobile devices, the principle of mobile-first (or even mobile only) should be the basis of any communication strategy. Meaning, companies need to prioritise mobile users, programs, and platforms in their business and communications strategies.

People have become accustomed to using their phones for everything, which has changed human behaviour. We have every answer at our fingertips through our smartphone, which means in all facets of life people want you to get to the point faster, because attention spans have decreased and a bite-size mentality prevails. Mobile use is supposed to be flexible in terms of time, so those who want to be successful must therefore be there when the user pops online. In addition, you must channel the required funds into the right media channels, of course.

In fact, penny-pinching when it comes to new forms of marketing is completely ludicrous. Vast sums are still being spent on TV and newspaper advertising when that industry communicates more or less the same way it did 50 years ago. These decision-makers have not yet grasped that people's communication behaviour has changed dramatically. In a nutshell, most companies are still running TV ads even though viewers are looking at their smartphones during commercial breaks.

As an agency, at Digitalscouting, we actually do produce TV and streaming ads. In fact, we just recently won a big campaign. We take the budget, but we don't produce a traditional piece of content that looks like an advert. And we tell that to our clients. We take your money, but we don't do what you want. We produce content that does not look, smell, or taste like advertisement. We produce media that looks like organic social content people know from social media. This sort of video has to be produced, edited, and scripted differently.

One particular insurer called us the Friday before Christmas for a campaign starting in January. They called us because the original agency messed up. And we are known not only for our attention-hacking strategy but because we can complete mission impossibles. I am not sure if they called because we are fast, or because we are radical. In the end we produced one of the most successful social media campaigns in recent insurance industry history in that market. That was fun for sure.

KLM as a Role Model

The Dutch airline KLM can be considered a role model for the expansion of touch points and digitally scaled communication. Passengers receive important updates on their journeys, and while they are still leaving the plane at their destination, a WhatsApp shows them which conveyor belt their luggage is on. If a problem should arise, KLM can easily be contacted via Twitter. Problems with bookings are dealt with in a straight-forward manner.

Offline Is Not Dead (It Just Doesn't Play a Central Role Anymore)

Even in times of smartphones and social media, some target groups still need a more personal touch. Just as we meet in person as private individuals despite WhatsApp and Face-book, digitally successful agents or insurers also network in traditional ways.

In fact, old-school, face-to-face networking is vital. Personal contact always opens up significant business opportunities, and this is true of everything from individual agents to large insurance groups. Our digital presence is only the tip of the iceberg. Behind the scenes, our in-person network determines whether we learn about the successful strategies of others or find promising partners.

Those who neglect friendships and acquaintances will eventually find themselves alone. This is all the more applicable when you are competing with other attractive offers. An in-person network, as the cornerstone of a sustainable company, needs appropriate nurturing.

Now ask yourself: when does a business partner or an industry insider help you? When they trust you and they know that they will also benefit from you. You need offline events and a permanent presence on social media to build this trust. Both aspects are interdependent and actually strengthen each other, and this principle is clearly evident in appearances at events. After all, this gives you the chance to present yourself and your expertise. The best way to do this is through presentations and speeches.

Why You Need to Give Speeches

Being a speaker has two distinct advantages. Recordings of captivating speeches and standing ovations not only look good on social media, but you also receive direct feedback at the event. If you give a good speech in front of 1,000 people, the five to six people who are passionately interested in your solution and your products will exchange ideas with you after the speech. So after your speech, stay right by the stage or very close to the auditorium! Be present at the event for at least another 2–3 hours so that your future clients, partners, or employees have the opportunity to approach you and exchange business cards or digital contacts.

At each presentation, invite participants to follow you on social media and to contact you at the conference if they are interested. As a speaker, you considerably increase the odds of finding interesting people in the sea of participants. VIP and speaker rooms, especially at international conferences and events, can be used as a retreat to meet up with others. If you see each other more frequently, invaluable relationships can develop.

However, the show does not end with your appearance on site. On the contrary, it is crucial to promote your speech. Do yourself a favour. At the next event and conference, take recordings of the event and ideally of yourself too; then caption and publish them. When you think about it, you can use image, sound, and text snippets in a myriad of ways.

Here are five ideas for your next event:

- Take a selfie the moment you book the ticket and share why you are participating and what you are looking for. Tag speakers you like to hear and ask who else in your network is going.
- Take great photos and write a summary of the conference, and include a list of five things you learned.
- Record and share your keynotes and panels.
- Conduct (micro-)interviews at the event.
- Produce high-quality videos.

Top Consultancies as a Negative Example

I notice again and again that partners and senior consultants of big consultancies jet off to conferences and events and leave the room and the event right after the speech. Decision-makers therefore have no way of approaching the speaker.

Nigel Walsh, long-time partner at Deloitte Digital (UK) – now Google Insurance – is an exception. Thanks to his continuous participation in, and many contributions to, the international insurance industry, he has become one of the top insurance influencers. Nigel stays on site after his talks.

You Don't Need Expensive Equipment

As the main purpose of this book is to provide practical value, I would like to briefly discuss the topic of technology. After all, videos, podcasts, and so on have to be made somehow. The good part is that nobody needs expensive equipment to start. Just use a decent smartphone. Apple phones have the advantage that their apps use customised drivers for photo and video capture, which is not always the case with Android devices. Due to the large number of Android cameras, standard drivers are often used. As a result, high-quality cameras in Android devices produce fairly average images. That's why we recommend Apple phones for capturing and processing photo and video material for social media.

Here are some more specific tech tips:

- For photos and movies, we use the Sony A7 III (with AF 35mm F.18), often with the Zhiyun Crane or DJI Gimble for smooth shots while walking and filming.
- For interviews we use a YC Onion Slider.
- The microphone we use is a DJI microphone or simply a Rode.
- Due to improved mobile phone cameras, I use a DJI OM 4 as my mobile phone.
- Thanks to its low weight and versatile applications, we use the Drone DJI Mavic Mini.
- For our professional Hollywood-like videos we have professional equipment and camera staff. But to start, the items listed here will do.

There is a disadvantage to the fact that you don't need a US$250 camera to start shooting a clip. A lot of people can, and do, do it. So, you are competing against a flood of content. While in the past it was enough to have expensive equipment and know the gatekeeper (media), now your content needs to have a minimum quality (a bar that continuously rises), and you need to have a high-quality inner structure and high content value. If you don't have that, it does not matter if your equipment was expensive or not.

However, even more important than superior quality is that you appear authentic and deliver exciting content and produce it in a format that captivates your viewers. With an expensive commercial on prime-time TV, you will at best attract attention for a short time. If, on the other hand, you are always present and offer cool content, you will be able to cement yourself permanently at the forefront of people's minds with even cheaply produced mobile videos.

Chapter 5

How Attention Hacking Works

E veryone receives over 13,000 brand and advertising messages every day; this includes online ads, TV ads, billboards, and more.

With people being bombarded with all this messaging, it's no surprise that a letter or phone call from an insurer gets forgotten, and the customer can be overwhelmed with lots of thoughts in their time of need – just none of these thoughts are of insurers.

In addition, only 2% of sales take place at the time of initial contact. In contrast, 75% occur between the 8th and 12th contact. In other words, insurers and agents have to contact their customers 8 to 12 times by phone, letter, in-person visit, or TV commercials. That's expensive.

Today, contacting customers is a lot more efficient because the insurance industry can produce relevant content in a modern format and distribute it on channels where the customer spends their time. Think of a short-form video on a social media channel instead of a TV ad. A large quantity of relevant content on the right channels should get consumers thinking about your brand at the time the need arises – and not about competitors. So try to stay at the forefront of people's minds. The more contact is made, the greater the likelihood of a purchase. The central objective underpinning your work is therefore to increase the number of touch points!

That is what attention hacking is all about. By making more frequent contact and higher-quality contacts, you improve your chances as a solution provider. You become part of the customer's world and thus automatically the contact person in times of need.

Attention hacking makes it possible for sales activity to be separated from the activity of individual employees. In the past, sales were mainly about the number of salespeople you had, but today sales figures can be increased even without increasing personnel expenditure. However, you have to do a lot before that happens. So bear in mind that it is about much more than just clicks or views. Attention hacking is a different way of thinking that puts the customer at the centre.

This approach applies regardless of the channel in demand; you can apply this strategy to new channels that arise in the quickly changing media landscape.

How to Reach Your Target Groups

If you want to make the most of your opportunities with attention hacking, you should first clearly identify the right target groups for your market.

From Customer Agent to Global Expert

In 2013, I started to work at a large insurer in their management programme, ultimately working as an insurance agent.

Today, decision-makers such as the chief regulators, board members, Insurtech CEOs, or worldwide superstars like Gary Vaynerchuk, Grant Cardone, Guy Kawasaki, and Rachel Cruz are guests on my LinkedIn live show and part of my network. When I am on stage, I am often introduced as someone 'who doesn't need an introduction'.

The majority of my clients approach me proactively because I am perceived as a top influencer in the industry. This is all thanks to attention hacking. The same mechanisms we'll talk about in this chapter work for managers and employees in operations and sales.

These may include any of the following:

- Existing customers
- New customers
- Sellers such as agents and brokers
- Sales managers
- Marketing/corporate communication
- Board members/decision-makers
- Potential partners

You should now add your own personal knowledge to this simple list. For instance, ask yourself: What makes your sales managers stand out? What interests does your potential new customer have? What points do you use to reach new business partners?

You know these questions from your previous work, but they also crop up in attention hacking. A list like this precisely defines the target groups, and it can serve as the basis for attention hacking.

Before you actually get started, you should work out the right time for communication. You have to be present when the customer wants to buy a house or car and has insurance needs. Those who do sales in the traditional way almost always phone at the wrong time. On the other hand, continuously generated attention ensures the salesperson learns of the individual need through constant contact. Attention hacking benefits the relationship with existing customers and puts you on the radar of new customers.

Don't believe that social media is only useful for targeting end customers! Potential can also be leveraged within your own company or in your own sales structure. For example, maybe your agents use LinkedIn and your salespeople are avid WhatsApp and YouTube users. Use social media to engage with your employees and colleagues better and faster.

Social Media Changes and Simplifying Your Work

The use of social media should not be an annoying side effort to your existing effort to gain new customers. Some of your previous efforts will be replaced and even simplified because roles, job descriptions, and self-image in the industry are fundamentally changing.

Think of the traditional work of a broker or agent manager. They currently visit two or three agents or brokers daily, each of them once or twice a year. The agent has a similar experience with the end customer. Phone calls, emails, and visits shape communication. However, this way of working is outdated and very expensive.

We can do better! Digital channels offer extensive opportunities to communicate more sustainably and efficiently. With video content (not only video calls) the agent supervisor ensures a permanent presence with partners and can anchor content much better due to the higher frequency. They then 'visit' all 50 to 350 sales partners every day. They can also supervise a lot more colleagues.

The situation is similar for the agent. Instead of four to five appointments per day or week, they get on the radar of hundreds or thousands of clients almost every day. We also know that more contact points in sales increase the likelihood of a purchase dramatically.

Our experience also shows that agents hardly ever respond to content produced by the central marketing department or by advertising agencies on the basis of outdated viewing principles. Instead, agents and end clients respond primarily to material that their supervisors or agents have produced for them. Therefore, the combination of traditional sales management and attention hacking are key to scaling the touch points with one's agents and end customers.

How to Be Heard as a Decision-Maker – Bypass Middle Management

Boards and executives can use social media to make it very clear what they stand for and where they are heading – and also to bypass middle management that sometimes block or water down projects. The messages reach the entire company and are not limited to meetings with the next management level.

However, experience shows that many board members need media coaching, social media help or a workbench that delivers content. The risk of triggering adverse reactions with a clumsy post is too great. Moreover, board members should – for some time – post themselves. This is the only way to develop a feeling for the channels, and authenticity is *the* currency as an influencer. There is nothing wrong with delegating this to staff later and to involve experts from the outside when your own staff does not have the expertise.

One of the world's best-known social media stars and successful serial entrepreneur and investor, Gary Vaynerchuk (if you don't know him, Google him and listen to at least three of his latest podcasts or vlogs), advised decision-makers and agents in the insurance industry in one of our programmes to:

> Invest time in trying out new apps and voice skills and produce content yourself, so you really get to understand how it works and you don't judge technology from hearsay but from your hands-on experience.

Nice Side Effect: Sought-After Experts Strengthen the Insurer

During a client project, we found that after only a few months of positioning on social media, management were getting people excited about the company and its transformation project – people who would previously have been unlikely to switch to an insurer. Among them were highly sought after IT and business intelligence professionals.

Furthermore, such positioning, paired with serious internal change projects, supports long-term employees who strive to move the company forward.

Meta-Strategy for Marketing Managers

So far, this chapter has been about individual attention-hacking principles for negotiators, decision-makers, and marketing managers. What is still missing is the level of positioning of insurers in general. Social media activities should always be internationally focused – even if an insurer is active in only one country. I call this strategy 'playing outside the lines'.

Unfortunately, sometimes users in Germany are very reluctant to give positive feedback. The situation is completely different in the rest of the world. There you will receive positive feedback far more often. At some point, your media presence on a topic will be so great internationally that your local or national journalists and market observers will no longer be able to ignore you on your topic, even if this means challenging the traditional hierarchy.

Key multipliers in the background play a special role, and these are often international. If they know and respect you, they will report positively about you openly and behind the scenes. If you produce German- and English-language content, the extra effort definitely pays off!

Chapter 6
Knowledge Is Not in Short Supply

I n this chapter, you will learn:

- That you should go back to your roots
- Why you can use your knowledge about people
- That there are very logical answers to your key questions
- What treasure lies buried in your company
- Why you should engage with Robert Kiyosaki
- The business fields you have not even thought of yet

Do people find insurance sexy? No! That's why we have to produce content that at first glance has nothing to do with it. We'll focus on topics like lifestyle, mobility, and safety in this chapter.

Those Who Help Will Be Helped

The insurance industry has a huge strength that we often forget about. We have an enormous quantity of knowledge about matters that interest our customers on a daily basis. We could help people by providing information on health, assets, and finances. However, we bury this knowledge in the depths of our organisations and forget to share it with our customers in convenient forms and channels.

Make the concept of helping others the guiding principle of your actions – whether at the company level or as an individual agent, agency, or decision-maker in the sector. In doing so, you will fulfil the most important condition for success in attention hacking – you will share your knowledge. This way, you can cement yourself in the minds of your target groups and be present the next time they need you.

However, for you to actually provide assistance, you need to answer four key questions, which you are probably aware of from your daily marketing practice:

- **What motivates your customers?** What private and professional issues are your clients concerned about? Look on social media to see what your customers are talking about. Analyse the app stores to see which apps are downloaded most often (for example at appannie .com) and find out which articles get the most clicks. You will notice that people are very interested in the topics we deal with. They just don't identify us with them.
- **What channels hold the attention of your target groups?** Maintain a realistic view of the channels and stop all investments in channels and formats that your target groups no longer significantly consume. This applies to television and Facebook. Do you want to approach young new customers or existing customers?

You have to use the channels and formats that your target groups currently consume. Simple as that.

- **How do you get this attention?** Two topics are of interest to people: information and entertainment. The details of a policy are nothing to write home about! The latest feature in life insurance does not answer the question of how long a person has to work. Firstly, we have to deliver content that is of interest to customers. Secondly, people want to be entertained – why not by us?
- **What format is suitable?** Nobody reads 80-page white papers. People prefer easily digestible and short content that gets to the point quickly. The most frequently used button on Netflix is 'Skip credits'. In addition, the format should fit your target group. When developing formats, do *not* take inspiration from your own or a neighbouring industry, but from the current media stars and media formats that are successful. Look at role models like MrBeast, Red Bull, or TheSoul Publishing firm.

Attention Hacking Works

My company has won some big industry accounts – including global players such as IBM, because we were at the forefront of decision-makers' minds at the moment of need. As a young agency (founded in 2017), we suddenly found ourselves on short lists, surrounded by traditional consulting firms. Many decision-makers wanted to give the young upstarts a chance. We then used this to establish ourselves. We also got attention because we were identified with the specific solution to a problem. We achieved this because we are continuously present on the relevant channels and present our solutions and successful implementations within and outside the industry. In doing so, we don't just write technical articles, we encapsulate that knowledge in thousands of graphics, podcasts, videos, and posts on social media and newsletters – and we do it completely free of charge.

Attention hacking is mainly about helping other people for free and not keeping information to yourself as a secret. There will be people who like to absorb this knowledge, apply it, and are successful with it. This has frequently happened to us and that's okay. Many people, however, are looking for very specific support in applying the principles to their particular situation and in implementing them. Then the decision-makers approach us. This principle can be used to generate more or new business for end customers – for example, by supporting your community.

Several of our clients saw the value of attention hacking – whether in B2B or B2C. One was super unhappy with its new business – growing between 1% and 3%. With attention hacking they achieved after 24 months year-on-year growth of 10% over several years. They did this without building up their own attention-hacking capabilities but by focusing on their core strength. We took over the concept, production, and distribution of several digital channels and parts of the sales process. Sometimes it can make sense to outsource it all.

Therefore, it is natural for me to pass on knowledge and tips free of charge. This type of investment pays for itself, and many sellers understand the principle behind it. People consciously and unconsciously prefer to do business with people they trust and like. People like those who help them selflessly and will come back to them at the moment of need. This principle helps the insurance industry because it is well-versed in areas where many people need assistance, including:

- Physical fitness: leading a healthy and long life
- Financial fitness: building, managing, and maintaining wealth

- Family fitness: protecting family and loved ones
- Spiritual well-being: fostering emotional security and good mental health.

Even if it seems like a stretch, household insurance actually has a lot to do with securing individual or family assets. For example, we know which activities or situations are dangerous and lead to damage. A home insurance company could provide tips on preventing water damage, like regular inspection of plumbing systems, proper landscaping to avoid water pooling near the house, or installing water leak detectors. They could also advise on fire safety measures like regular inspection of electrical wiring, proper storage and usage of flammable materials, or installation and maintenance of smoke detectors. Educate your followers about this and help avoid insurance claims from the outset!

Financial Freedom: An Opportunity for the Industry

Insurers can provide expertise in key areas of life. They know the strategies underpinning money management, wealth accumulation and maintenance, safe investments, and financial freedom. They know exactly how and why people become wealthy. This knowledge provides numerous points of contact for helping the public – especially since there is great demand! After all, people make pilgrimages in droves to Robert Kiyosaki, Dave Ramsey, or Grant Cardone. Why don't you take inspiration from such successful business models and advise your clients?

Fortunately, some insurers are already starting to take advantage of the opportunities available. They use their extensive knowledge to become the clients' 'go-to' person.

This opportunity is independent of assets, family, and professional circumstances, age, or other general conditions. We can help almost everyone achieve their goals. Our industry can become a partner in areas such as security, lifestyle, and wealth, just as Amazon is to shopping, and Apple is to mobile phones.

Such a strategy of partnership continuously cements the insurers at the back of the minds of the respective target groups. We gain attention by means of providing useful information. We have to think about how we can be of assistance. This is how to gain trust and, as a result, future opportunities. While insurers should continue to sell products, the motivation to do so must totally change. We need a new self-image! With the right content and visibility in the appropriate channels and formats, the insurance industry can become a strategic partner in people's lives.

Claims cost us a lot of money. Why don't we change this? With our extensive knowledge of the insurance industry, we can help customers identify losses before they even occur. Why don't we empower consumers to reduce claims? The insurance industry knows the dangers of using technology, being in one's own home or out and about on the street. Even health data can be found in abundance in the archives of insurers. Those who disseminate this information in a targeted manner and provide their customers with real help will not only find open ears, they will also reduce their loss ratio in the long term. These ideas are perfect for an extensive campaign on all available social media channels.

In addition, claims settlement is the moment of truth for the relationship between the customer and insurer. Those who can show goodwill with lower expenses will win in the long term.

Part II

Implementing Attention Hacking

Now we have arrived at the practical part. In 10 well-defined steps, we will show how you, as a salesperson, decision-maker, and marketing manager, can implement the principles described earlier internally in a very practical way to achieve your main goal – to establish yourself permanently on the customer's radar. To do this, you should proceed step by step. These are the 10 simple tasks we'll talk about in the following chapters:

- Set (unrealistic) goals
- Get started on the right foot
- Engage your community

- Use suitable formats
- Digitally scale offline events
- Be where the customer is
- Become a content machine
- Identify your relevant influencers
- Build social media into your daily routine
- Build an effective sales funnel

Chapter 7
Set (Unrealistic) Goals

S ocial media, the Internet, and attention hacking are – as previously discussed – not ends in and of themselves. They are tools that can be used to achieve a goal. However, applying all these principles is pointless if you haven't set your overarching goals. Here are some examples of goals:

- Sales growth
- Increase in profitability

Increasing the quantity and quality of contact points with customers and partners leads to increased engagement with target groups. This increased attention leads to customers and partners to think of your company at a time of need. This, in turn, increases turnover and profitability, as this type of marketing and sales is digitally scalable. Unlike in the past, the increased activity does not trigger linear cost growth. In fact, when existing budgets are reallocated, there may even be an overall cost reduction.

Attention Hacking Fires Up Sales

One of the most influential brand and sales changes in recent years has undoubtedly been implemented by Lebensversicherung von 1871 (LV1871). At the DKM 2018 industry trade fair, visitors almost didn't recognise the stand due to the radical brand transformation. This repositioning led to an overarching and holistic transformation process. A little later, the long-established insurance company was considered one of the freshest brands on the market. This new image, in turn, had an impact on connecting with partners and attracting new employees and customers. LV1871 now regularly delivers growth bucking the market trend in a crisis-ridden line of business.

Interview with Thomas Heindl, head of marketing and corporate communications, LV1871

Why did you decide to modernise your brand as part of a major transformation process – from branding to broker support?'

This question cuts to the heart of our strategic focus. Today, a brand is no longer just a brand. The boundaries between marketing and sales are becoming increasingly blurred. Therefore, it was not just about repositioning the brand but about laying the foundation for the sales transformation. With the consistent digital alignment of the brand, we were also able to launch a changed form of B2B2C sales, stronger digitalisation of interactions between sales and business partners, all the way to social selling.

How did sales develop in recent years?

We have seen significant growth in new business over the past 3 years. Contrary to the market trend, the contribution total for new business increased further in the 2020 financial year (by 8.8% compared to the previous year). The recorded gross contributions have risen by 3.6%. The current income from contributions grew by 1.8%.

How to Define Goals

At the beginning of projects, I am sometimes surprised that some of my clients do not define any overarching goals or visions alongside their specific sales objectives. As a result, employees and partners don't know what direction to take. Defining goals is as easy as following these simple steps:

1. Have a detailed and rigorous external analysis of the current situation (including strengths and weaknesses) carried out in advance, including internal and external interviews, audits of external appearances, documents and internal plans.
2. Get expertise from third parties, such as from the most respected insurance experts around the globe who are friends of yours, or consider hiring someone to help.

3. Define goals based on broad data. This is not about painting castles in the sky or wishful thinking; it is about defining unrealistic goals and visions that motivate the organisation to think the unthinkable and try the impossible.
4. Formulate specific projects and measures to achieve these goals. I am always surprised that the more non-committal the steps are planned, the higher up in the hierarchy we carry out this process. However, any planning needs realistic and firm deadlines and defined responsibilities.
5. Start with the implementation. Continuous pushing and supporting are by far the most important points for change to really happen.

Unrealistic goals unleash forces.

One of our clients, a traditional insurance company, declared an unrealistic goal internally. Sales doubled within 5 years. At first the staff were shocked, but now every decision is evaluated according to whether it contributed to the achievement of this goal.

Chapter 8

Get Started on the Right Foot

B efore you post on social media, take a close look at the channels that are relevant to you and study the behaviour of your target groups. Take your time and make notes. Make sure you do the following:

- Observe the content that the people post for a few days/weeks.
- Analyse what content is successful and what is not so well received.
- Reflect on your own reaction to the posts and write down the reasons for them.
- Identify the opinion leaders and multipliers.
- Try to find out the prevalent opinion.

These tasks do not involve any magic tricks. It is about developing a sense of the habits and preferences of the customer. If you know 'your' channels well enough, you can get started yourself.

The previous tips also apply to people who are already successfully using some channels and would like to become active on more of them. TikTok is a case in point. Even as long-time professionals, at my company we had to learn from scratch when TikTok was released. With any new channel, you need to systematically examine it before your first post.

Toolbox: Just Upload!

We make mistakes, too. For several months I heard Gary Vaynerchuk almost begging to finally get started with TikTok. I got started only half-heartedly. Then my team begged me. Instead of looking into it more intensively, I made the same arguments as the old decision-makers in the industry. I was in the wrong. So in the summer of 2020, we started a structured campaign on TikTok.

First, we uploaded some videos from other channels. We thought it was a great secondary use of material. What time we saved! We soon, however, noticed that there was a lack of responses and reach. The existing videos didn't work on the new platform.

You will be doomed regardless of whether you have good content or not if you ignore the specific features of the channel. Since we have been producing films explicitly for TikTok or adapting existing ones, the views and likes have been in the millions. Don't make our mistake, take action that is suitable for the channel in each case!

Don't Waste Time!

The biggest mistake of my professional career was waiting 7 years between coming up with the idea for Digitalscouting and launching my company. I always wondered whether I should go ahead with the project, what others thought about it, how successful it could be, and much more. Avoid these mistakes and get started now. You already know more than enough, so put the book down and write two or three posts now.

Why not take a selfie with this book, write a (hopefully) positive comment about it, and post it on a channel that is important to you? (While you're at it, also feel free to write a review on Amazon. Thanks!) Maybe something else is on your mind. If so, process this through! The main thing is to start now and get the positive experience of having taken the first step.

I mean it. PUT THIS BOOK DOWN and post NOW.

I'm not joking.

You will thank me later. (You can treat me to dinner at Trattoria Calabria in Hamburg-Eimsbüttel or to a bottle of gin.)

Use the momentum.

While you're still riding the high from the first post, you should make a plan right away. What do you want to post during the next 3 days? What specific topics or events are particularly suitable for this? Here, too, you can follow some established steps:

1. Comment, share, or like the content of others – especially influencers.
2. Create your own content and work toward getting other users to share your content.
3. Create your own content in which you interview third parties. Incidentally, this can also be used for sales purposes.

If you work for a company, please refrain from working out strategies for years at a time. Otherwise, you will be like many others in the industry. You think about Facebook for

15 years and then go live when the platform has long since lost its appeal and is basically dead. Social media is fast moving, so work accordingly. Medium-sized and smaller players have it easier. If there is good leadership, they can start without extensive coordination rounds with multiple levels of sign-offs.

Here are three mistakes you want to avoid to survive:

- **Mistake 1: Doing it on the side:** Attention hacking is not something you can do on the side. The strategic introduction of new channels in our industry often fails because visibility is decided from the top. Yet, employees at the operational level are supposed to do a 'little bit of posting' on the side. Every decision-maker should know that creating good content and publishing it in a smart way is a new part of the core activity in operations, staff, and sales. Or to put it in the words of a Swiss sales executive, 'We no longer take on anyone who can't or won't do it – regardless of what they've done in terms of sales.'
- **Mistake 2: Forgetting about it:** Even highly motivated employees fall off the wagon. This happens when their operational and target-driven day-to-day work consumes them. Therefore, managers should clearly define, for their employees and for themselves, how many hours per day and week they should spend on this new activity. It won't work without blocked out time in the calendar.
- **Mistake 3: Trying to reinvent the wheel:** Some companies really want to find out everything themselves. But, breaking news – sometimes it's easier to get help from the outside. Find experts with a proven track record and let them become your outsourced marketing or social media department.

Mark It Red in the Calendar

At Digitalscouting, we helped one of our international clients in an operational sales unit responsible for bancassurance. The goal was to increase the frequency and quality of contact between the insurer, the responsible sales team, and bank employees by means of digital content.

Even though managers and staff were noticeably passionate about the project, it threatened to fail several times. There was no opportunity in the packed daily sales schedule to take the content collectively produced to the banks.

The solution was that we blocked out time for coordination and communication in all calendars. Attention hacking is not something that is done as an add-on; it changes the way we work.

Chapter 9
Engage
Your Community

You know your goals, and you have done at least a trial run. Now we are getting to the nitty-gritty – taking a closer look at the different players in social media. Broadly speaking, a distinction can be made between two different groups:

- **Actors and multipliers:** There are always engaged people who shape opinions in a particular community. Many of them are not necessarily target customers – on the contrary, they will never buy anything. Yet, they influence the purchasing decisions of our target groups.
- **Viewers and consumers:** Keep an eye on users who only consume. However, if they make tentative attempts at communication, they make significant contributions and develop a relationship with content creators, and potentially also with you. Even if this group does not say much, your work there can really pay off.

TikTok is only for the young? Not at all!

I sat down with the head of sales of a large German insurer and his sales managers. We discussed how we could turn several thousand sales staff into micro-influencers. At the end of the conversation, one participant said: 'Now I know where I know you from. You're on TikTok!' He had consumed my content there – but had never written a comment or introduced himself. He was just a viewer. Nevertheless, my activity led him to associate me with positive things. In a not-irrelevant B2B sales conversation with decision-makers aged 40+, a presence on a social media platform was suddenly a plus. The outcome of this conversation alone made the entire investment in developing our TikTok channel worthwhile.

Particularly in our industry, the split between influencers and viewers is often deeply entrenched, with many people holding back permanently. However, we believe that the number of views in the financial and insurance environment is often very high, but usually there are only very few likes or shares. When it comes to clothing, sports, technology, or similar, you can expect significantly more activity. However, this is no reason to panic.

The logical response is to expand your topic scope to include infotainment and entertainment!

Those who publish or share harmless, funny, or entertaining content that is still professionally relevant and substantiated usually receive more feedback. By doing so, it is easier to enter into an actual exchange and build a substantial relationship with people. Engagement means nothing other than actively building a relationship with members, actors, and multipliers. (Note: It is not necessarily a matter of turning these people into customers! Instead, the community should perceive you as a reliable contact person and expert on specific matters. This is the goal you should strive for with actors and viewers.)

Interview with Klaus Hermann, insurance broker and Germany's premier insurance entertainer

You combine insurance topics and humour like no one else in Germany. How does this combination work?

It works great! On the one hand, I entertain my colleagues in the industry with talks, videos, moderation, and cabaret. Many enjoy seeing the proverbial mirror being held up to the industry. Humour is truth and pain. Why stop at the insurance industry? I am convinced that when the insurance industry does not take itself too seriously it has a positive impact on people outside our profession.

Should agents and insurers be allowed to publish content that is humorous?

Oh, yes. Definitely. As long as it's done in good taste. Making fun of clients' insurance claims on Facebook stories will likely generate a shitstorm. Misadventures and funny stories from the office, on the other hand, convey humanity and a sense

(continued)

(continued)

of closeness. But beware, not everyone is naturally funny. What someone does should always be true to their nature and not seem forced.

What is your advice to insurers and agents?

Be bold, different, and unexpected. Try it out, think the impossible and take small steps, but always move forward. Take our industry seriously, of course, but don't take yourselves too seriously. Have fun and spread joy at work and be serious about it.

Tips for Insurers and Marketing Managers

I have already outlined relevant matters for the insurance industry, but the aim here is to break them down for individual players in more concrete terms. At the level of the industry as a whole, we also need to address issues that really affect people and share our knowledge that is relevant to them.

- Life insurers could join the debate on financial freedom and the accumulation, preservation, and expansion of wealth. Why don't insurers help their customers build wealth over the long term and adopt behaviours and strategies that make this possible? We are, after all, more serious than the majority of business and get-rich-quick gurus. But they reach millions.

- Property insurers could make their knowledge and technology even more accessible for the prevention of damage to the home, company, and car. Why doesn't my insurer send me a message when a storm is coming, so that I can put my car in the garage? This would also be good for the loss:cost ratio.
- Health insurers and health insurance companies can take advantage of the fact that fitness, health, and wellness are booming. Insurers, such as Deutsche Familienversicherung (DFV), are among the first to address these issues by publishing relevant content tailored to their customers' needs. When it comes to dental care and dental diseases, no one can ignore the DFV articles on the Internet. The industry could really expand this practice. Why shouldn't the best fitness, wellness, or weight-loss programme come from a health insurer?
- Insurers as employers: Insurers repeatedly complain about not being able to recruit enough junior staff or experts. Suppose you, as an insurer, let your employees have their say and pour the content into exciting formats appropriate to target groups and channels. This would allow you to position yourself as an attractive employer.
- Brand: In addition to very specific stories, an overarching branding meta-story can also be created based on the systematic application of attention hacking. Those who produce continuous, relevant, and authentic content will not just reach their target groups; those who go further than the rest of the industry are perceived by the market, the media, and the industry as being more modern, fresher, and more future-proof. These strategies work. After all, we all know insurers and agents who have a presence in the market that is disproportionate

to their size. What they all have in common is that they communicate more than others do and opt for new formats and channels. They do things differently and more often than others tend to.

Tips for Agents

Whether it is a large broker, a large tied-agent organisation or an individual agent, all sales units can focus on specific topics and appropriate formats as well as permanently place themselves on their target groups' radar. In doing so, they have four crucial advantages over insurers.

- Agents do not need to reach millions of people. Instead, contact with a few hundred or thousand people in the region or segment is often enough to ensure a steady stream of new business.
- Self-employed agents have more freedom to share very personal content and blend their private and professional content.
- Thanks to their independence, agents can get started almost without needing to coordinate with their distribution partners. Here, being small in size is an advantage that allows you to gain speed.
- Many agents have local roots and an exciting network. This may be crucial because partners can be involved in content creation.

Allianz representative Volker Büscher achieved a high level of engagement because he not only talked about his work but also about his dog. His Facebook presence is one of the widest reaching of the blue giants in Germany.

Potential topics for posts include:

- Authentic stories about customers. Don't just show successful claims settlements; you also need to address the very core of our industry and how we help our customers in their darkest hours. It is often the agent who first rushes over to the local entrepreneur when his business is on fire. He hands over the first emergency cheque before the fire brigade has finished extinguishing the flames.
- Your client portfolio, which includes many exciting stories. Why not interview engaging customers and put the conversations online?
- Interviews can also be an exciting new customer recruitment model. Ask local entrepreneurs about specialist topics and give them the insurance booklet later!

Without a strategic background, I publicly outed myself early on as a fan of Hamburg Sports Club (HSV) – precisely at a time when the association was generating almost nothing but negative headlines. Apart from some well-meaning taunts, decision-makers kept talking to me about HSV. There were also customers for whom the mutual proximity to HSV and the shared suffering as fans paved the way for a business relationship. What hobby could you share?

Tips for Employed Sales Managers

One of the biggest levers in sales is to transform the activities of salaried sales managers. It goes without saying that phone and email enquiries should be responded to. However, sales managers can also increase the frequency and quality of contact by using their own content on social media.

- Founding of a micro-sales academy – the manager compiles the best sales tips from experience and share them with fellow agents.
- Weekly podcast – instead of making dozens of phone calls, all you need to do is record a voice message with the week's most important news and issues. They get instant updates from agents via Messenger.
- Newsletter – send the most important information and tips by email.
- Interview the best agents from your division with a focus on practical tips and tricks for fellow colleagues.

Fun fact: You don't need to develop social and digital selling academies and transformation programmes yourself. And if you do so, it's hard. Why? Because it's not easy to transfer knowledge into strong sales organisations and change the way the majority of the staff works every day. The good news: We have social and digital selling academies and change programmes immediately available. We have clients whose sales teams have increased their contact points with their clients and leads 10–40 times. I surely don't need to tell you as a sales and marketing professional what that means for the sales success. It skyrocketed.

Document your work – selfies and beautiful photos from the everyday life of a sales manager add a human touch. Sales managers can increase the frequency and quality of contact by creating relevant content for their own agents. They can also attract new agents and account managers by sharing content on social media.

Tips for Board Members and Decision-Makers

Behind closed doors, many decision-makers lament rarely being able to reach individual staff. However, it is the direct line that counts, especially in transformation and growth projects. In addition, board members and other leaders also have career aspirations. They often realise that they and their achievements are unknown outside the company and a small group. This limitation hinders negotiations on follow-up contracts or changing jobs. Therefore, decision-makers in particular should be professionally active on social media.

There are several good role models in Germany, who we will take a look at later. The following list gives some suggestions to decision-makers for raising their profile:

- Continuously clarify, explain, and reiterate the vision, mission, and strategy of the company and board.
- Positively highlight staff and team who have gone above and beyond to achieve these goals.
- A look behind the scenes of board meetings.
- A look behind the scenes of the company.
- A glimpse into your private life.

Address the 95%

Ma Mingzhe, founder of Chinese insurer Ping An, found out in the early 1990s that the Chinese would probably never spend more than 5% of their income on insurance. It didn't matter how hard the company tried. Ma decided not to settle for that and decided to build a group that offered targeted products and services to channel a larger part of the remaining 95% of his customers' budgets onto his group's balance sheet. He systematically added new products and services to the value chain. Ping An is now the

(continued)

(continued)

largest insurance company in the world, depending on the criteria.

Ping An is an impressive example because it is not a venture-capital-driven tech start-up from Silicon Valley but an ordinary insurer, with a visionary and bold decision-maker.

Chapter 10
Use Suitable Formats

L et's start with the good news. Communication formats have not changed in the past thousand years, with a few exceptions. Humans communicate using sounds, images, and text. New communication, storage, and distribution formats, on the other hand, are cropping up regularly. The long list of formats includes cave painting, letterpress printing, radio, and motion pictures. Now, digital storage and distribution capacities are crucial.

Choose the Right Format

You want to use the best format for the job.

Images

Each target group and channel has specific aesthetic and content preferences. For you, this means defining these preferences with respect to your goals on the basis of systematic and substantial testing and analysis. Afterwards, you can produce images that strike a chord with your target groups. However, you can kiss goodbye to the idea that at some point, you will have understood exactly which images and visual language your target groups prefer. Preferences change all the time. Some insurers do not understand this and continue to produce images and imagery that have not reached anyone for 15 years and sell this internally as a proven strategy. While professional images and graphics used to be expensive, modern programs and online services make it possible to create images that are tailored to the target group and channel with little effort.

Use online tools if possible and create images using the same means as lifestyle and sports influencers. Sometimes it takes longer to start established programs such as Adobe Photoshop than it does to semi-automatically produce a photo with a template in Canva.

For our client LPP we combined super high-quality Adobe photos and well-made videos with quicker produced content with Canva. Can you tell which post was created with which software?

Videos

While films like Doctor Zhivago captivated millions of viewers in their cinema seats for hours, such successes are inconceivable today. Go and have some fun and watch your favourite film from your youth or that of your parents. I bet you will find the film lengthy. Videos today follow different structural rules. While the dramaturgy used to increase slowly after an introduction, today the climax is at the beginning – followed by several other highlights. Today's audience mercilessly punish content they don't like. Viewers simply click away or watch other content. With their almost infinite choice of options, video and streaming services have raised people's quality expectations. We have to take that into consideration. That's why it's so important to produce a lot of videos. This is the only way to determine what content and structure will be well received.

Not to forget ChatGPT (that went mainstream at the beginning of 2023) – a conversational tool powered by artificial intelligence (AI) enabling regular users to use a sophisticated tool without developer skills. You just type in your request and the AI generates a unique text. On the one hand it's a great tool that lowers the bar for people to create content. On the other hand, the lowering of the bar of good content will increase the bar for high quality. So if everybody – even without writing or picture-editing skills – can generate content, the demand for obvious handmade, well-written, and valuable content will increase. So in the short term I urge everybody to apply AI – in the long term we all need to increase our creative skills (or hire an agency to do so).

Meanwhile, there are programs like Beatleap that can create high-quality videos within seconds and are driven by AI. With just a few minutes of post-production, videos are created that, in the past, would have taken teams days and a six-figure budget. Of course, it may still make sense to increase production expenses with drones, lighting, and professional editing, but background noise is possible today with small budgets.

However, one thing is for sure. If you really want to stand out, you need to increase the quality of your storytelling and content concept and the quality of your production. While in 2019 it was possible to impress with a one-shot video, now good videos need several scenes, good lighting, and decent cameras. To start, it's okay to go with a mobile phone and low-budget software, but nowadays audiences demand high-quality content. In addition, the algorithms demand a high quantity of well-made content.

Text

'Do you even read these anymore?' I asked an insurance executive friend, pointing to a stack of newspapers. 'No, but they look good when visitors or board members come.' An honest answer! After this revelation, I took a closer look at the printed material in the offices of the company's decision-makers. There was never a crease in the spine of magazines, studies, or brochures. Furthermore, what is read and what gathers dust is constantly changing. Nowhere is this development more evident than on the Internet, where reading time and visitor numbers can be tracked with clarity. Don't produce texts 'the way we've always done it', but use content that is in demand for you and your target group.

Audio

The potential of audio content is massively underrated. The unique charm of podcasts, audio news, voice devices, or even platforms is that audio can be consumed without having to look at the medium. When driving, flying, or jogging, you have your hands free. Depending on the profession, audio content can even be consumed while working. As a content creator, you benefit because you are very close to your target group and have the attention of your customers. It doesn't get much more intimate than that.

Think About the Target Group

When developing your content, it is crucial that you determine precisely who your target group is and their actual preferences. Based on this, you can develop a combination of audio, video, image, and text formats for your specific audience. The following formats are doing particularly well for us and our customers:

- Giving interviews or conducting interviews with stars or the target group.
- Articles on trends and developments.
- Classification of general trends with regard to the importance of the industry.
- Regular content series.
- Reports from events and conferences.
- Selfies taken at events or everyday occurrences related to the target group.
- Stories about private hobbies.

But avoid anything negative. Make no negative comments about competitors or people who attack you. Rise above it. You are welcome to make fun – as long as you do it about yourself. Develop and experiment with your own ideas.

The Problem of Superstars

At the beginning of the coronavirus pandemic in March 2020, my company decided to use the crisis as an opportunity. Instead of reducing activities, we increased them significantly.

This included the launch of a live broadcast on social media – first daily, then weekly – with entrepreneurs, board members, and Insurtech and insurance experts. The reach and exposure of the guests accelerated so quickly that, 9 months later, we had several global superstars on our show: Gary Vaynerchuk, Grant Cardone, Guy Kawasaki, and Rachel Cruz (if you don't know any of them, please quickly Google them).

Normally we bring well-known guests onto the show in different 6-month periods, but we had to publish them within a few weeks to accommodate all their different schedules.

Attention hacking is always about turning events into media events. Whether you're attending a conference, giving a talk, visiting customers or doing something else, think about how you can spread the word about it on social media. For example, announce in advance that you are attending a conference and provide a little animation to accompany the post, take a selfie on the way there, broadcast a short live video with the most interesting facts from your attendance, do interviews, and so on – produce lots of images, videos, and text. Remember to combine entertainment with interesting information.

Leveraging ChatGPT and Other AI Tools for Content Creation in Social Media Marketing

The rest of the chapter was initially generated by AI using this request (edited for publication):

Create a 3,500-word chapter on how to use ChatGPT for content creation (finding ideas, researching, using ChatGPT for writing texts, posts). Include potentially viral examples for the insurance and banking industry for each channel:

Instagram, LinkedIn, TikTok, and YouTube. Also mention and explain the top 10 AI-driven tools to generate pictures, videos, captions, as well as the top five ChatGPT chrome plugins. Please include five examples of how ChatGPT and other tools will change the way insurance sales and insurance headquarters will change in the future.

ChatGPT-Generated Content[*]

In the constantly evolving digital landscape, companies in the insurance and banking industries must maintain an active presence on social media to engage their target audience, drive brand awareness, and generate leads. However, creating fresh, engaging content can be a daunting task, especially for businesses with limited resources.

This comprehensive section will guide you through using ChatGPT for content creation, including idea generation, research, and writing texts and posts, with potentially viral examples for insurance and banking industries using Instagram, LinkedIn, TikTok, and YouTube. Additionally, we will introduce the top 10 AI-driven tools for generating visuals and captions, as well as the top 5 ChatGPT Chrome plugins. Finally, we will discuss five examples of how ChatGPT and other AI tools will change the way insurance sales and insurance headquarters operate in the future.

(continued)

(continued)

Using ChatGPT for Content Creation

Finding Ideas

Generating fresh content ideas is critical for maintaining an active and engaging social media presence. ChatGPT can be a valuable tool for brainstorming new concepts and themes for your content. Begin by defining your content goals, such as raising brand awareness or promoting a product, and provide ChatGPT with relevant prompts. ChatGPT will generate multiple suggestions based on your prompts, allowing you to identify ideas that resonate with your brand and audience. You can further refine these ideas by providing more context or specific requirements.

Research

To create informative and engaging content, you may need to conduct research on specific topics. ChatGPT can help you gather relevant information from various sources, analyse the data and extract key insights to include in your content. You can provide prompts related to your research topic, and ChatGPT will generate responses that can serve as a starting point for your research or help you validate existing data.

A fun way to start is to ask ChatGPT: 'I want to generate viral posts on platforms like LinkedIn – what prompts should I use?'

Writing Texts and Posts

Once you have your content ideas and research insights, ChatGPT can help you create engaging texts and posts. Specify the platform you are creating content for, such as Instagram, LinkedIn, TikTok, or YouTube, and determine the tone and style you want for your content. Provide ChatGPT with detailed prompts that include the desired tone, style, platform, and content theme. Review and edit the generated text to ensure it aligns with your brand voice and meets the platform's character limits.

Potentially Viral Examples for the Insurance and Banking Industries by ChatGPT

Instagram

Insurance Example 1: Create a series of 'Insurance Myth-buster' posts, debunking common misconceptions about insurance policies. Use eye-catching graphics and concise captions to engage and educate your audience.

Banking Example 1: Launch a 'Money-saving Monday' campaign, sharing weekly tips on how to save money and manage personal finances more effectively. Use visually appealing images and

(continued)

(*continued*)
informative captions to provide valuable advice and promote engagement.

LinkedIn

Insurance Example 2: Share a series of thought leadership articles on emerging trends in the insurance industry, such as the impact of AI, climate change, and remote work on insurance policies and risk management. Use compelling headlines and well-researched content to establish your brand as an industry expert.

Banking Example 2: Develop a series of case studies highlighting your bank's innovative solutions to common financial challenges faced by businesses. Use engaging storytelling and data-driven insights to showcase your bank's expertise and build trust with your audience.

TikTok

Insurance Example 3: Create entertaining and educational TikTok videos that simplify complex insurance concepts, such as 'The 3-Minute Guide to Home Insurance' or 'Understanding Life Insurance in 60 Seconds'. Use humour and creativity to make the content engaging and easily digestible for viewers.

Banking Example 3: Produce a series of TikTok videos featuring 'Life Hacks for Financial Wellness', offering tips on budgeting, credit management, and investing. Use engaging visuals, animations, and short informative captions to capture your audience's attention and encourage them to share the content.

YouTube

Insurance Example 4: Develop a YouTube series called 'Real-Life Insurance Stories', featuring customer testimonials about how insurance policies have positively impacted their lives during challenging times. Use emotive storytelling and high-quality video production to evoke empathy and reinforce the value of insurance.

Banking Example 4: Create a YouTube channel dedicated to financial education, offering tutorials on various topics such as savings strategies, understanding credit scores, and investment basics. Use clear explanations, engaging visuals, and real-life examples to make the content accessible and relatable for your target audience.

Top 10 AI-Driven Tools for Visuals and Captions

In addition to ChatGPT there are other AI tools that can help you. Here are our favourites:

1. *Canva*: Canva uses AI to provide templates, colour palettes, and fonts based on your preferences

(continued)

(*continued*)

and requirements. Its AI-powered design assistant also generates design suggestions for your social media graphics.

2. *Lumen5*: This AI-powered video-creation platform helps you transform text or blog posts into engaging videos for social media by providing suggestions for images, videos, and music.

3. *DeepArt.io*: DeepArt.io uses AI algorithms to turn your photos into digital artwork by applying styles from famous paintings or custom styles.

4. *RunwayML*: RunwayML is a creative toolkit that uses machine learning to generate visuals, allowing you to create unique images, videos, and animations for your social media content.

5. *Pikwizard*: Pikwizard is a stock image library that leverages AI to provide personalised image recommendations based on your searches and preferences.

6. *Artisto*: This AI-powered video editor helps you create captivating video content with a wide range of artistic filters and effects.

7. *Visme*: Visme uses AI to assist with infographic creation, presentations, and other visual content by providing automatic layout suggestions, colour palette generation, and font pairings.

8. *Pictory.ai*: Pictory.ai converts long-form text into summarised videos with automatically generated visuals, captions, and voiceovers.

9. *Tailor Brands*: This AI-powered branding platform helps you create custom logos, social media graphics, and other brand assets based on your preferences and brand identity.
10. *Caption Pro*: Caption Pro is an AI-driven caption generator that creates relevant, engaging, and platform-specific captions for your social media content.

Top 5 ChatGPT Chrome Plugins

As well as apps and websites, there are chrome plugins that facilitate ChatGPT:

1. *ChatGPT Assistant*: This plugin allows you to access ChatGPT directly from your browser, making it easy to generate content ideas, answer questions, and create text without leaving your current tab.
2. *ChatGPT Summariser*: With this plugin, you can generate summaries of long articles or web pages, making it easier to gather research and create content based on your findings.
3. *ChatGPT Grammar Checker*: This plugin uses ChatGPT's language understanding capabilities to check your content for grammatical errors, ensuring that your social media posts are polished and professional.

(continued)

(continued)

4. *ChatGPT Translate*: This plugin enables you to translate text between multiple languages using ChatGPT's language understanding capabilities, making it easier to create localised content for your global audience.

5. *ChatGPT Keyword Generator*: This plugin helps you identify relevant keywords for your content, improving your search engine optimisation (aka SEO) efforts and increasing the visibility of your social media posts.

How ChatGPT and Other AI Tools Will Change Insurance Sales and Insurance Headquarters in the Future

- *Example 1: Streamlined Claims Processing*. AI tools, such as ChatGPT, can help insurance companies streamline claims processing by automating tasks such as document analysis, data extraction, and fraud detection. This could lead to faster claims processing times, improved customer satisfaction, and reduced operational costs.

- *Example 2: Personalised Customer Experience*. ChatGPT and other AI-driven tools can help insurance companies deliver personalised customer experiences by analysing customer data and providing tailored product recommendations, pricing, and communication strategies. This could lead to increased customer loyalty, higher conversion rates and stronger customer relationships.

- *Example 3: Enhanced Risk Assessment.* By leveraging AI tools like ChatGPT, insurance companies can gain deeper insights into risk factors and assess risk more accurately. This could lead to better pricing strategies, more accurate underwriting and a more efficient allocation of resources.
- *Example 4: Virtual Assistants for Sales and Support.* ChatGPT and other AI-driven chatbot technologies can be deployed as virtual assistants to help insurance sales teams and support staff. These virtual assistants can assist with lead generation, qualification, and nurturing, as well as providing real-time support for customers, reducing response times, and improving overall customer experience.
- *Example 5: AI-driven Training and Development.* ChatGPT and other AI tools can be used to develop personalised training programmes for insurance sales teams and support staff. By analysing employee performance data and learning patterns, these AI-driven training programmes can provide targeted learning experiences that

(continued)

(continued)

address individual skill gaps and improve overall team performance.

As the digital landscape continues to evolve, businesses in the insurance and banking industries must embrace AI-driven tools like ChatGPT to stay competitive and maintain an engaging social media presence. By leveraging ChatGPT for content creation and utilising AI-driven tools for visuals and captions, businesses can generate unique and engaging content tailored to their target audience. Additionally, Chrome plugins can further enhance the content creation process by providing added convenience and functionality.

The examples provided here, for potentially viral content in the insurance and banking industries across Instagram, LinkedIn, TikTok, and YouTube, serve as a starting point for businesses looking to create engaging and impactful social media content. As AI technologies like ChatGPT continue to advance, their applications within the insurance and banking industries will expand, leading to more efficient and personalised experiences for both customers and employees. By embracing these emerging technologies, businesses can position themselves for success in an increasingly competitive and digitally connected world.

* This content was edited slightly for publication.

Chapter 11
Digitally Scale Offline Events

Do you want 100 or 184,000 viewers?

You can facilitate the reuse of content by planning strategically. For example, I structure my talks and interviews so that 10- or 20-second snippets containing the most important information can easily be taken from them afterward. You can also do this with presentations, workshops, or other events. Identify suitable content that can be used on social media in advance and ensure that it can be easily edited.

Selfie or Recruitment Ad?

Together with one of our clients, we tested whether a glossy job advertisement or a selfie of the boss in front of a computer screen with a job advertisement would achieve a wider reach. The selfie had five times the reach. Since then, the company has consistently published announcements for events, products, or job vacancies with selfies instead of professionally posed shots. This example shows that even a boring job advert can be turned into a small media event, and its reach can be increased by serving a primal human need for faces.

Forget Direct Viewers

There are no longer any fully offline events. Events and conferences are primarily media events – for you as a participant or, even better, as a speaker. It goes without saying that it is pleasant to meet people and listen to presentations at a conference or an evening event. However, it is even better if you produce content at an occasion your viewers value. It becomes genuinely profitable when you publish the resulting content on channels where your viewers feel at home and in a form that appeals to your target group. This may include selfies from conferences with a high-quality content summary of the day or well-made videos and interviews. Suddenly you will not just reach the 14 people at the event, but 14,000 or 140,000 by means of the content you created for the Internet. Still not convinced? Simply multiply the cost of a conference visit by 1,000 or 10,000 to get a similar contact rate.

That's pretty expensive. You save this cost by following the tactics suggested in this chapter. It is almost silly to go to a physical event – whether as a speaker or a visitor – and not exploit it as a media event online. Being able to reach a multiple of those present should be a strong enough argument for making the leap.

Many events in everyday life are also suitable for media dissemination. Did you see something unusual or did you experience something special? Post about it!

Who Needs Phone Books Anymore?

A few years ago, I walked past a large stack of phone books ready to be thrown away. I snapped a photo of them immediately and shared it with the question, 'Who still needs phone books today?' It got a huge response! In the future, always walk around with attention hacking in mind; everyday situations can often be relayed in the form of news or entertainment. Repeat the mission and vision over and over again.

A difficult change in mindset is how you relate to yourself. Every influencer sets themselves up as a media person. They have to come out of their shell, tell and share stories, show personal presence again and again, and take responsibility for this publicity. In my experience, it comes down to no longer separating private and public life. Once you have made this decision, you will never run out of content. I exclude anything that is too personal, such as family events and things of that nature. However, one thing is clear: if you are not prepared to reveal anything about yourself, you can't tap into attention hacking.

If you post frequently and provide a detailed account of your activities, you will create feedback effects. Ten videos and posts from your appearance at a trade fair bring additional publicity to the organisers. Other organisers are then more likely to invite you because they know about your engagement. The same applies when you document how you visit companies. Post about it and advertise the company at the same time. Finally, one more warning. Don't use the General Data Protection Regulation (GDPR), Insurance Distribution Directive (IDD), Markets in Financial Instruments Directive (MiFID) and the like as an excuse to produce boring content or to have no presence at all. The following are a few examples of how to digitally scale an event.

Before the Event

A lot of posters are posted before an event while traveling or release a graphic provided by the conference and/or the event itself. The latter happens especially when you are a sponsor or speaker. For a lot of events and decision-makers such graphics are great because they can be published quickly and provide reach for the event. An example follows.

It is even better if you generate your own authentic content. This could be a selfie from travelling or while preparing the conference. Also share what you are expecting from the event or what you are specifically seeking. For further effect generate content with someone else. The example following is a picture of me with Stefan Riedel. He is not only one of

Posts

Dr. Robin Kiera · You
Let's hack the attention of your customers with modern sale...
2d · 🌐

#Secret meeting revealed.

Stefan Riedel of codecentric AG and I met last week - and we were super excited that insureNXT conference in Cologne is taking place next Wednesday and Thursday.

I am expecting

- Great meetings with great minds of the industry
- Inspiring keynotes and panels
- A great afterparty Sebastian Pitzler promised during the pandemic

See you in cologne

Stefanie Asbe, Konrad Bartsch, Gerald Böse, Alexander Braun, Florian Bremer, Joséphine Chamoulaud, Moritz Delbrück, Dr. Sylvia Eichelberg, Alexander-Otto Fechner, Florian Graillot, Nina Henschel, Sven Jantzen, Anna Kessler, Sebastian Langrehr, Anina Lutz, Thomas Lüer, Carsten Maschmeyer, Torsten Oletzky, Andreas Popp, Dr. Xenia Isabel Gioia Poppe, Nicole Schepanek, Thomas Sattelberger, Andreas Schertzinger, Jürgen Sprang, Sabine VanderLinden, Stephen Voss, Oliver Weigelt, Melissa Wong

the nicest and most knowledgeable people in the industry but also one of the best known. So combining his and my reach we helped the conference with a post more appealing than a selfie graphic post.

For your unique position it could make sense to publish a picture of you, your team, or your company attending the event. Make sure you tag speakers, sponsors, and friends you want to hear or meet at the event.

During the Event

Creating posts at the beginning of the event not only gets you reach in your industry but also motivate people to contact you. So instead of you looking for people to meet and help with your products and services, people – who wanted to talk to you anyway – approach you.

This actually happened to the co-CEO of Digitalscouting Katja and our new sales manager at a recent HR conference. They posted the following post at the beginning of the conference and four different people approached Katja, a well-known expert in the HR industry, and wanted to chat.

Dr. Katja Kiera · 1st
Geschäftsführerin Employer Branding & HR Transformation
5d · 🌐

Lernen und Networking @Zukunft Personal #hamburg

Mit unserer neuen Vertriebsexpertin Rosa le Claire. Wir sind sehr glücklich, Dich an Board zu haben!

Wir freuen uns auf einen spannenden Tag und nette Gespräche.

Wer ist noch da?
Was dürfen wir nicht verpassen?

Valeriy Leibert Carolin Laue Laura Beste Anika Krüger Anke Ruhnow

#networking #lernen #messe

See translation

Interviews

Become a thought-leader platform. A super-smart way to provide value to the whole industry is to conduct interviews with decision-makers, multiplicators and key people in the industry. We have done this for years. We started it to provide the people at home – who could not travel to the event and not speak to the industry VIPs – with an opportunity to air their point of view on industry topics.

One side effect was that a lot of decision-makers actually enjoyed our fun interviews and several became clients and customers in the following years. The conference organisers really enjoyed well-made, fun, entertaining, and knowledgeable videos that also promoted their event.

The following graphic shows an interview that was part of a series at the German DKM conference, probably the most important and biggest in the German insurance industry. We have been a media partner of that conference for years. I had the privilege of interviewing Michael Franke, one of the best-known entrepreneurs in the industry and also one of the hardest to get an interview with.

Dr. Robin Kiera · You
Let's hack the attention of your customers with modern sales, marketing, ...
3d · 🌐

🚀 It's a game-changer! Modularity offers more flexibility and customization for the #insuranceindustry.

...see more

Thought Leadership by Summarising

We live in times of extreme overflow of information. So if you organise and evaluate information people are happy and consider you a thought leader. So if you – after an event – summarise the most important, three, five, or seven points, you provide value to the visitors and to those who were not able to attend.

When creating a short but valuable text we always add graphics illustrating the points presented and/or pictures of the event. These must be well-designed to be accessible and impactful.

So you see, an event can provide topics and posts that can reach thousands of people online. It helps you to attract the attention of decision-makers and the love of the event organisers.

Dr. Robin Kiera · You
Let's hack the attention of your customers with modern sales, marketing, ...
6d · 🌐

🚀 Bigger, Better #Insurtech! Sharing exciting lessons from the recent Insurtech Insights event.

There were over 5,000 attendees at the Intercontinental Hotel at the O2 Arena in London, and the energy was absolutely electric!

Here are 4 Key Takeaways.

Insurtech's next evolutionary stage is a revival.
The ecosystem remains enormously strong, the service and technology providers, in particular.

Evolution instead of revolution.
Incremental improvements in existing processes, business models, and technologies, are the common denominators among the solutions. I agree with Florian Graillot of astoryaVC, one of the best French VCs and influencers, that this is only the beginning.

Physical sales and marketing are not an issue – not yet.
There is still room for improvement in the way brokers and intermediaries communicate.

DACH shone with its absence.
I'm hoping to see more decision-makers from Germany, Austria, and Switzerland next year!

You can also read the article thru the link in the comments. 👇

Our sincerest gratitude to Versicherungsbote for publishing. 🙏

Gunnar Lange, Sabine VanderLinden, Stan Nazarenko, CFA, Lisa Wardlaw, Ed Halsey, Uy Nguyen, Dietmar Kottmann, Frank DESVIGNES, Richard Sachar, Pasquale Caterisano ⚡, Mark Windy, Simon Baldus, Jochem Schueltke, Florian Schubert, Nikolaus Häufler, Olivier Dot, Tim Leberecht, Jörg-Tobias Hinterthür

digitalscouting – Marketing, Sales, Strategy, Social Media, Speaking.

#insurtechinsights #insurance #innovation #sales #europe

Chapter 12

Be Where
the Customer Is

Attention hacking calls for the right channels. What used to work on television or in magazines now works mainly on social media. This is not a static slab of rock with clear rules, though – everything is in flux. Today, LinkedIn, WhatsApp, YouTube, Twitter, and TikTok are highly suited to the insurance industry, as are Xing, Facebook, and Instagram to a limited extent. Experience shows, however, that this list will look different in 5 years or even 5 months. What always matters is where people's attention is at any given moment. Go to the places where people are looking for answers to their questions right now.

Do not listen to public opinion or your marketing agency's results on which app is best. It is because demographic groups outside the core target groups of new platforms rarely admit that they are already using these apps – even though they spend hours on them. Trust the download figures instead. Discreetly look at your target groups' mobile phones on buses, trains, and in public and find out which apps they use. This insight can be more useful than expensive market research.

If a platform grows less rapidly or even stagnates, its appeal usually also decreases. As a rule, there is more content than users – the supply increases more than the demand. This means that organic reach decreases. You reach fewer and fewer users with the same quantity of content. The reason is simple: platforms need to restrict or monetise access to content because users would otherwise be inundated. A positive side effect is that they can now charge money for this reach. For example, on some Facebook pages, the reach has dropped to below 3%, and only a fraction of fans see the posts and articles in the newsfeed, even though they have liked the page.

You should also never forget that the different target groups of a company can cavort on different channels. Therefore, let your engagement be guided by the specific product and the communication strategy that goes with it. However, the principle is similar across channels, strategies, and target groups. Social media are used to target people previously not reached by means of attention hacking. There are two key objectives here, with which you are already familiar:

- People should approach us of their own accord when they need insurance.
- We would like to have the contact details (phone and email) so that we can approach people.

The second point is a challenge. This is because Twitter and the like are pursuing their own commercial goals and want to exploit the potential of their users, first and foremost, for themselves. They act as gatekeepers and want to keep our interaction with other users on their platform.

Direct social media users to their ecosystems, such as the company website. There they are expected to leave their telephone number and email address and this facilitates direct contact. This creates a community independent of third parties and reduces your dependence on transient platforms.

> To become part of the Digitalscouting community, please register here: www.digitalscouting.de/whats appreminder

No one will take away the telephone numbers and email addresses of customers, partners, or decision-makers that you have accumulated. Your primary goal is to obtain this data. Attention hacking is merely a tool for this.

Insurers and agents need direct access to their customers, decision-makers to potential partners, sales managers to their employees, and companies to (potential) employees. Adapt your homepage design so that it cultivates these contacts, collects data, and develops lead magnets! However, you need to give your target group good reasons to pass on their contact details.

> Access to the customer is your gold!

In my experience, LinkedIn, YouTube, TikTok, and WhatsApp are the most important channels.

At the beginning of Digitalscouting, we focused on LinkedIn and Twitter – also for resource reasons – and neglected Instagram, although we achieved a relatively high level of engagement with my private account. When we started to use Instagram systematically, the days of organic reach were gone in most parts. However, we are currently still having very good experiences with the story-and-reels feature.

In the following sections, you will find facts and figures, an overview of your first steps, dos and don'ts, pro tips, and must-watch profiles specific to each channel. Added to that, there is potential content. Regardless of the channel, you should always be mindful of privacy, copyright, and data protection.

Dealing with New Surges

When the user numbers of our TikTok channel exploded, we suddenly had hundreds of thousands of views per day. We also used this to boost our other, more established channels. We called on Tik-Tok users to follow us on Instagram and LinkedIn as well. As a result, our customer relationship management collapsed within a very short time due to thousands of messages via Instagram. Due to this exponential growth, we were only able to assign colleagues to answer these questions after a few weeks.

Thousands of Instagram and hundreds of LinkedIn messages undoubtedly created problems. But our conscientious response to respond to almost every message then laid the foundation for the success of a whole new line of business: selling fashion on TikTok. How did this happen? The influx of audience interaction highlighted a potential interest in fashion, and our brand's success in building engagement and trust set the stage for launching a fashion line. Utilising TikTok's visual platform, cross-promotion across other social media channels, and its growing e-commerce capabilities, our company effectively harnessed this opportunity, turning overwhelming audience engagement into a thriving fashion business.

This story shows how new business opportunities can arise by chance.

LinkedIn

Here are some facts about LinkedIn (per `www.omnicoreagency.com/linkedin-statistics`).

- LinkedIn has more than 310 million active users per month.
- 57% of users are male.
- 6 out of 10 users actively search for industry information.
- The average income of a LinkedIn user is just under US$47,000 per year.
- LinkedIn is the most important B2B.

Here are the steps to get started on LinkedIn:

1. Create a compelling profile with a professional image.
2. Make sure the main banner incorporates your corporate colours.
3. Integrate high-quality content into your profile to highlight your skills. This could be articles, speeches, or studies.
4. Find suitable evidence of your expertise to adequately document each professional milestone. This will give visitors to your profile practical insights.
5. Follow people you find interesting, and like and comment on their content. Engage with others!

Some of our clients really like kick-starter help. So we conduct audits and deliver a fixed set of graphics and videos. Some clients need support in building up their own teams, others give us the mandate to conceptualise, produce, and distribute their content.

Here are some dos and don'ts:

- In a lot of countries, almost no one believes employer references anymore. So you should not publish them on LinkedIn. Rely more on articles by you and reports about you. Social proof is crucial!
- Every employee of your company should have a background banner with the corporate design.
- Use hashtags, even if they don't generate a lot of traffic at the moment.
- Tag: Only use the @ feature with users you really know, and from whom you can expect a positive reaction! They will be informed via the notification feature.

- Discount codes and conference announcements achieve little reach.
- Don't keep going on and on about your product!
- Share your company's vision and mission so that they are made clear to your employees, applicants, and customers.
- Experience has shown that the sales function tends to annoy readers. So don't overdo it with the Sales Navigator on LinkedIn.
- Scheduling tools such as SocialPilot or Hootsuite allow you to write posts in advance and publish them automatically at set times. However, it is currently not possible to tag people with @ using these tools. So you can schedule posts, but then you have to edit them manually.
- LinkedIn is not keen on LinkedIn profiles being processed by third parties. So if an agency or employee is actively managing your account, this should be done from the same or similar IP address. Anyone who ignores this rule risks being blocked.
- Content performs well when it contains a personalised touch. So don't only post news, but post your personal opinion on the matter.
- Face, face, face counts. It makes all the difference if you post a PDF of your annual financial statement or if your CFO looks into the camera, smiles holding the report in their hands. In our experience, posts that include faces of real people reach 4 to 20 times more people.
- Video, video, video: There is no doubt that we see the TikTokisation of LinkedIn. So we see a flood of short videos with strong storytelling aspects of it.

Content That Works on LinkedIn

On LinkedIn, the focus is on your professional expertise. It therefore makes sense to post and link to your articles, interviews, or contributions in magazines. Occasions for reports and discussions include conferences, trade fairs, or when you visit another company. Some background noise can be created with news – just write briefly what moves the industry and perhaps add your commentary. Thank-you notes are also well received, as are personal statements, so take advantage of opportunities. Report on your business trip, announce your own appearances, and share your life with others. Keep it down to earth though, self-congratulation tends to have the opposite effect – unless you put your customers or staff in the spotlight. As on other channels, authenticity matters on LinkedIn.

Here are some pro tips:

- Include your brand name and logo in the profile picture because many other channels and platforms automatically download these images and use them for events, for example. This way, you will strengthen your company brand at the same time.
- Use the featured function and attach high-quality content directly to your profile. This way, you provide supporting evidence of your expertise at a glance.
- Instead of your job description, use a call to action with your USP. For example, I write 'we make your customer come to you'.
- Incorporate your articles from trade magazines about you or by you, they have a high level of credibility and therefore highlight your status and position in the industry.

- Create your own content. For example, interview well-known colleagues about an interesting topic and post the interview. This is how you create content and get into conversation with others.
- Videos have a wide reach – as long as you include the links from YouTube. Organically uploaded videos get less reach than YouTube links.
- Since LinkedIn does not deliver posts to all users, you can repost the successful posts after a month or two and then reach other users.
- Tag opinion leaders and those people (for example, relevant existing customers or leads) who absolutely need to see your post.
- Post at least two to three times a week. Ideally, do so once or twice a day.
- Titles with 40 to 49 characters work best.

My Must-Follow Profiles on LinkedIn

This list is not exhaustive. The profiles mentioned serve as examples, there are many more we could have included.

Martin Gräfer: The board member of DBV provides incredibly authentic insights into the company's activities and clearly positions DBV on political issues as well. Instead of urging agents to train, he posts his own training certificate.

Christopher Lohmann: As a former board member of Talanx and HDI, he delivers incredibly engaging, as well as unscripted, authentic insights. This gives the impression of an accessible board of a group worth billions.

Interview with Christopher Lohmann, former board member of Talanx and HDI

Christopher, what was the deciding factor for starting on social media back then?

In all honesty, I can't even remember the exact moment. A few years ago, during the development of Gothaer's employer branding, I noticed how important social media is in terms of the perception of a company as an attractive employer or not. Keeping an eye on review platforms and taking them seriously plays a role in this. After all, we can't ask our representatives to systematically manage their Google reviews and then ignore services like Kununu. In addition, it is important to make the social aspects of companies visible to the outside world on social media. This is also, and especially, the task of those who are responsible.

A good two years ago, I started to actively use my then dormant LinkedIn account for my own posts – and I rediscovered my former joy of (journalistic) writing. It's a win-win situation, right?

You not only share official company information or professional contributions but also provide insights into your work as a board member – why?

Well, social media is about human and interpersonal interaction, that's what makes these media social. Simply posting company news or facts does not do it justice. Therefore, in my posts, I make a point of making clear my reference or opinion on the topic I am writing about. I find it completely normal and only human to leave questions unanswered sometimes because I don't have all the answers. In our VUCA world, I am suspicious of people who think they have – or seem to have – the right answer to everything and everyone. When it comes to feedback, I also notice that my readers want to view me as a human being. I get a lot of feedback on this, especially on personal stories, for example, when I couldn't get my hair cut because of coronavirus, or on my first day at work at HDI – a hot 1 August, a Saturday, when I said 'Guten Tag' to the porter in Bermuda. It's not difficult for me, I'm just like that, and apparently, that's how it comes across 'out there'.

What was the most significant event of your online presence on LinkedIn and the like in the last 12 months?

I remember the post where I publicly announced that I was leaving Gothaer as being particularly significant. At the same time, I was not yet allowed to say that I was going to HDI for various governance and communication reasons. So I thanked Gothaer and made it public that I was looking forward to a fantastic new job, which I would write about in a few weeks. That's what I did. The post was read over 100,000 times, and I got hundreds of congratulations

(continued)

> (*continued*)
> on a move that no one knew how it would turn out. This showed me that people trust me after a year of posting on social media – and I didn't disappoint them. The reaction back then still touches me today, and it shows the power of social media when you are honest and authentic on it.

Lutz Kiesewetter: The head of communications at Deutsche Familienversicherung is its indefatigable voice on LinkedIn, sharing news of its achievements. He and DFV form an important hub of the international community.

Adrian Jones: The analyses of the senior manager at Scor are among the most well-established in the international insurance industry. He regularly picks up the financial reports of hyped Insurtech start-ups and asks the right, critical questions without being unfair.

Nick Gerhart: The US manager provides detailed insights into the US insurance industry, as well as into smaller use cases and players that are less well-known.

Steve Tunstall: One of the most connected insurance professionals in Southeast Asia. He shares interesting facts about the insurance industry there.

Nigel Walsh: Certainly one of the most likeable agents and experts in the industry. He was one of the very first influencers and his analyses are indispensable.

Thomas Rechnitzer: Senior manager at IBM, he ran major hybrid industry events both online and offline in 2020.

Pierangelo Campopiano: CEO Smile from Switzerland.

Jim Marous: One of the leading voices in Fintech and the US banking and finance industry.

Rob Galbraith: Best-selling author and veteran of the US insurance industry and global insurance influencer.

Kobi Bendelak: Former insurance agent and now CEO of InsurTech Israel. He is the face of InsurTech Israel around the world.

Denise Garth: Chief strategy officer at Majesco known for her profound industry analysis.

Florian Graillot: The face of the French insurance and InsurTech ecosystem and VC.

Sabine VanderLinden: One of the most well-known women in the international insurance industry with a profound knowledge of building start-ups and ecosystems.

Those are our top posters and what we can learn from them. Thanks to them. Those who thank others sometimes get a wide reach on LinkedIn. That has been my experience on all channels and in all formats.

YouTube

YouTube is a crucial platform for attention hacking in the insurance industry. Note: this is a search engine and not a social media platform with a feed (besides Shorts)! People use YouTube to find out something or to be entertained. If you want to be discovered, you have to offer relevant, high-quality content.

Despite the fact that YouTube is almost 20 years old, it still has some surprises left. Some said it had its climax and quickly, when TikTok threatened its position, YouTube quickly developed YouTube Shorts, also allowing new content creators onto its platform with a changed algorithm.

Goal: Your videos should rank at the top of searches for your keywords and provide users with answers to their questions.

Role Model: MrBeast

Why is MrBeast so super successful as the world's most successful (and fun, modest, and nice – in my humble opinion) YouTuber? MrBeast found entertaining topics and scaled videos to an extreme. So he organises competitions where people can win a million dollars or a luxury car if they don't leave a circle or if leave their hand by an object, like a private jet. One video is more insane than the previous ones. Nevertheless you can really feel how MrBeast and his team focus radically on the need and desire of their audience – reaching billions of people (no writing error, it's literally billions).

Here are some facts about YouTube (per www.youtube .com/intl/de/about/press):

- YouTube is the most commonly used search engine and the most visited site after Google.
- YouTube has more than 2 billion users. YouTube is available in more than 100 countries and 80 languages.
- More people already prefer video platforms like You-Tube, instead of traditional television.
- Over 70% of traffic comes from mobile devices.
- The most successful insurance channels in this country are HUK24 with just under 18,000 and Allianz with around 15,000 subscribers. US car insurer Geico, on the other hand, is followed by over 1.8 million people!

Here are steps to get started with YouTube:

1. Start watching YouTube videos and subscribing to exciting channels on specialist topics and other areas of life.
2. Keep a close eye on which videos YouTube shows you on the homepage and which videos are displayed for certain search terms.
3. An ecosystem exists for search engine optimisation.
4. Identify your focus points and the keywords that are useful for them.
5. Just start with your smartphone camera or use a simple digital camera.
6. Stay away from the Canon EOS 750D and similar cameras. Their mechanical autofocusing is so noisy that it ruins your videos (like it did for us in the beginning).
7. We initially worked with www.wevideo.com. This will give you good results. You don't need a professional video team to start with. But make sure to get one, as soon as you become serious on YouTube.
8. Publish your first videos as soon as possible and see what happens.
9. Gain practical experience with the medium of video and gradually enhance your proficiency.

Here are some dos and don'ts:

- Pick topics that others have not addressed or for which you can deliver better videos.
- Don't just look at channels for your topic! Browse through YouTube and analyse which videos and channels have many followers and views and what you spontaneously like. Note down the success factors in each case and how you can use them – adapted to the insurance industry.

- Write a mini video shoot schedule with the following questions:
  - What target group do I want to reach and engage with?
  - What reaction or action do I want from this target group as a result of the video?
  - What stories, information, and entertainment can I use to spark the interest of this target group?
  - How do I ensure that the user does not click away within the critical 0.5 to 3 seconds at the beginning?
- Prepare your content in a comprehensible way and avoid technical terms. If that is not possible, explain in a short sentence.
- Write meaningful descriptions for each video. Repeat keywords and terms that your target group may search for.
- Get to the point quickly and be concise. The first 3 seconds must work, otherwise people will click away from it.
- Give all videos appropriate hashtags.
- Create playlists for relevant topics.

Content That Works on YouTube

The most important question is: what would your customer search for in terms of a problem that you have the solution to? What keywords would they use? What question would they type into the search box or ask their voice device? The correct answer is what makes it possible for them to find your video in the first place.

Moreover, we have to make sure that they also watch it – preferably until the end. Even if it is to be about insurance and finance, you should focus on the quality and style of successful channels from areas such as entertainment and edutainment. Test to see which style features are transferable. Look for pertinent topics such as severe weather, seasons, or celebrity birthdays so that you can send your own messages about topics such as damage, appointments, or age. Note: YouTube is not the place to go into the small print of the insurance terms and conditions. On the contrary, you should help people with information about particular problems and, needless to say, entertain them at the same time.

Here are some pro tricks:

- The first words of the titles are vital for them to be found. If you want to touch on the topic of life insurance, the title should not be 'What is #TermLifeInsurance' but rather '#TermLifeInsurance – what is that?'
- Tools such as www.contentrow.com offer inspiration for good titles.
- Differentiate between topics that seem to interest your customers and those that they actually spend their time on. Hardly anyone admits to watching entertaining pranks, dance videos, or motivational speakers. However, the numbers speak for themselves. Cater to real interests!
- Design longer videos in advance so that you can publish short parts of them independently.
- Use YouTube as an archive for your videos and generate visits at the same time.
- Use tools like:

  - Amberscript (for automatic transcription)
  - WeVideo or (for video editing)
  - Tubebuddy (SEO) for editing and management.

Must-Watch Channels on YouTube

Here are some must-watch channels:

Casey Neistat: He has become a familiar face on You-Tube. Individual videos have 20 to 30 million views – with 12.2 million followers to boot. Insurers or salespeople can also be inspired by how modern videos are edited and how stories are told. Nevertheless, he never went all in like MrBeast.

Bayerische Staatsforsten: The visible passion on this channel is so infectious that individual videos receive hundreds of thousands of views – with the niche topic of forestry. Supposedly dry topics can inspire millions!

Geico: The US car insurer became well known thanks to its original advertising on TV and has transferred this principle to the Internet. For example, clips with a Neanderthal were successful.

Gary Vaynerchuk: He has moulded entire generations of marketeers and entrepreneurs on his Garyvee channel. The former Facebook, Uber, and Twitter investor not only shares practical tips, but also presents himself as an exemplary CEO. This allows him to act as a role model for decision-makers in the insurance industry. Gary Vaynerchuk has been a guest on our show twice. This can be found on YouTube and LinkedIn.

Grant Cardone: Every agent ought to know Grant Cardone. Although not everyone likes his tone, he is an example of how salespeople can pass on their knowledge in an exciting way. However, this requires good sales techniques and not just outdated sales manuals. We were able to get

Grant Cardone on a live broadcast, and this can be found on YouTube and LinkedIn.

Dave Ramsey: The United States' 'Mr Debt Free' has created a nationwide movement with his fight against consumer debt. Debt freedom, financial freedom and financial health are also relevant to us – insurers could touch on a few things here.

Our Best YouTube Posts and What We Can Learn from Them

With over 160,000 views, this was our most successful video: www.youtube.com/watch?v=CLHyPS6NS2k. The reason might be that it was one of the first videos to discuss trends in the international insurance industry for a year, and, on top of that, the first few seconds were a bit more provocative than normal.

This video showed a rather crazy week as an Insurtech influencer: www.youtube.com/watch?v=9jsfVoUfo5I. It received more than 40,000 views and generated follower growth for months. I think it was watched so many times because people are interested in getting a peek behind the scenes and it was also edited to be very fast-paced.

The video of the world's first end-to-end insurance purchase via Amazon Alexa at Deutsche Familienversicherung got 38,000 views on YouTube: www.youtube.com/watch?v=gr6fG78rOsk. Here, it was mainly the novelty and news value that led viewers to the video.

How US$15,000 Became Over US$24 Million

Simon Chiu, headmaster at Saint Francis High School in Mountain View, California, as well as some parents, had observed their children using this new yellow app. As a result, the school invested US$15,000. This yielded a profit of US$24 million for the school. The app was Snapchat.

Here are some examples of our own:

- As well as client channels we have two of our own. One newer B2C promoting financial literacy and a second B2B for the insurance and finance industry.
- On our B2C channel we had some successes with influencer interviews in the German YouTube ecosystem.
- We also take our insights into YouTube B2C content and apply them into B2B campaigns or content made for our corporate clients.

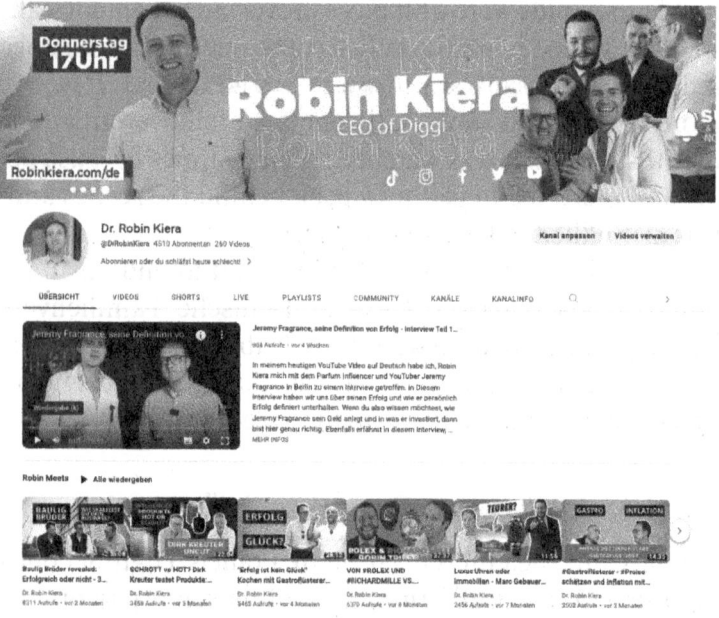

- We also designed and produced several YouTube performance marketing campaigns for large insurers. The secret there was that the ads we produced were not perceived as ads, but as organic content because we actually produced them as such.

WhatsApp Messenger

Alongside TikTok, WhatsApp is currently an insider's tip that should be looked into. Every company should have a Messenger or WhatsApp strategy! On this platform you will have the best-possible access to your target group. There are three major advantages. First, the high level of attention ensures that all messages are opened. Second, there are no adverts – yet. Third, almost no companies – least of all in the insurance industry – use WhatsApp strategically or for sales.

Goal: Get into people's private circle of friends and create optimal credibility and direct access.

Here are some facts about WhatsApp (per www.fortunly .com/statistics/whatsapp-statistics):

- WhatsApp has about 2 billion users worldwide.
- WhatsApp is available in more than 180 countries and 80 languages.
- More than 65 billion messages are sent per day.
- There are more than 5 million business users.
- Half-a-billion users use the status function every day.
- Users spend an average of 195 minutes on WhatsApp every week.
- WhatsApp is about private matters.

Here are the first steps:

1. Check whether you need to use WhatsApp as a private person or WhatsApp Business. The latter offers many features to support your marketing.
2. Add all the mobile phone numbers you know (where you have consent) to your phone.
3. Send a message to their contacts – something like 'Hello Jim, I found your business card in a drawer and wanted to send you my phone number. See you soon, yours XY.' If you receive a reply, you can add the contact to your broadcast lists.
4. Post selfies with short statements about your everyday life, customer stories, and personal stuff on your Whats App status at least once a day. A trick: clickable links can also be inserted in the text functionality. This allows you to send your WhatsApp contacts to other platforms. You will quickly see how many decision-makers are looking at what you are doing.
5. Segment your contacts by interests or target groups and build broadcast lists.
6. Join our WhatsApp community: `www.digital scouting.de/ whatsapp-reminder`

Here are some dos and don'ts:

*   Never add people who do not know each other.
*   Even hardcore fans may find too frequent use of the broadcast feature annoying. Therefore, I would use it a maximum of twice a month per person and with more distant acquaintances a maximum of once.
*   Use your best content.
*   Never bother private communities with advertising or job topics.

- Respect the GDPR.
- Despite any concerns you might have, don't miss out on this huge opportunity.
- Use WhatsApp stories and take note of who is watching you there.

Content That Works on WhatsApp

WhatsApp is a platform with a private focus, so stick to communicating more private matters. Use the channel for your business just as you would use it with your friends! For example, agents can report on their office day. Customer stories are often very suitable, for example explaining why an occupational disability insurance policy was taken out or how a claim can be settled on a specific object. But you can also use your visit to the stadium of your favourite club as an opportunity to create content.

Sales managers, for example, can post the successes of other agents, additionally some board members use the channel to share the status of projects or to keep the team in the loop. A discussion in groups is also often a good way to get a quick impression of the mood.

Here are some pro tricks:

- The WhatsApp broadcast function makes it possible to send messages to up to 256 contacts at the same time, and yet each recipient sees them as a private individual message.
- For example, you can announce live shows via broadcast and drive traffic to other social networks and positively influence their algorithms.
- Use groups to establish a professional exchange amongst like-minded people.

- Closely examine who is looking at your WhatsApp status and start a structured sales funnel with it.

We can't show our best posts on WhatsApp because they disappear after 24 hours. Basically, the absolute core of fans and followers check in regularly to see what Robin is actually up to.

Twitter

Twitter, the short message service, should play a key role in any internationally focused attention-hacking strategy. This is a good place to follow current developments and spot trends. Twitter is very relevant, especially at the international level. In some countries like Germany, the short message service didn't ever really catch on apart from amongst journalists and technology enthusiasts. However, influencers and some insurance executives are easy to reach, for example by retweeting them.

Our Twitter channel @Stratorob has over 43,000 followers and belongs to the top 20 most important Twitter channels in the insurance industry. A lot of rankings regularly identify me as influencer and thought leader as a result of our work on Twitter.

We have a whole team producing Twitter posts and we also reuse content we produce for other channels. In addition, we run channels for companies around the world with different target groups, reaching millions and millions of people each month.

Although Twitter is no longer central to our strategy, we reach several million people per month.

Here are some facts about Twitter (per www.oberlo.com/
blog/whatsapp-statistics www.fortunly.com/statistics/
whatsapp-statistics):

- 66% of Twitter users are male.
- Twitter has over 330 million active users per month.
- 500 million tweets are sent every day.
- 80% of use is on mobile devices.
- Nearly half of the users consume Twitter daily.
- 80% of Twitter users are affluent millennials.
- 93% of users are open to brand engagement on Twitter.

Here are the first steps:

1. Use a good profile photo.
2. Look at your competitors' channels and follow successful
   channels from other business sectors.
3. Follow international influencers such as:
   InsurtechNews
   DIA
   Insurtech Insights
   And, of course, www.digitalscouting.de
4. Look for relevant hashtags.
5. Retweet, like, and comment on content from target companies, target people, influencers, and multipliers.
6. Share content on Twitter as well – ideally 80% industry
   news and only 20% should be your own content.
7. In contrast to WhatsApp and LinkedIn, mass counts
   on Twitter – 20–50 or even 100 tweets per day are not
   uncommon – if you have something positive and interesting to say.

Here are some dos and don'ts:

- Use the right hashtags for your industry and products, and create company and brand hashtags.
- Make sure you are up to date! Outdated information has no place on Twitter.
- Stay away from political controversies.
- Pay attention to people who bring particular hashtags to your attention. Thank them and follow them. This is how occasional content consumers become loyal fans. We even employ designated staff for this purpose.
- A personal connection can be made with tags, for example @stratorob. Just be careful, only do this with people you know and can expect a positive reaction from! If you act too swiftly and frequently here, you might be seen as a spammer.

Content That Works on Twitter

Twitter in the insurance industry is highly news related. This includes professional news on the industry and products, interviews, live shows, rankings, and personal information. You can share this in the form of short statements and insert a link to further information; you can also include a video.

Here are some pro tips:

- Firmly cement your USPs at the top with a pinned tweet.
- Build closed groups of fans and thought leaders where you discuss content and share the best content.
- Have a call to action in your tweets.
- The reach clearly exceeds the number of followers.
- Scheduling tools such as Hootsuite, Buffer, or SocialPilot make it possible to schedule tweets and publish them automatically.

Our Best Posts and What We Can Learn from Them

On Twitter, we have never experienced content going viral when compared to other channels. Our high reach is based on only 20 to 40 relevant tweets on specialist topics every day. It's the quantity that counts! We achieve above-average reach with superstar guests or reports from conferences.

Examples: Use your face – also on Twitter. Even though we share content of tech topics and complex issues we always try to include my face. This is not to boost my ego – I know that my face qualifies me more for a career in radio than in TV – but posts with faces get 10–20 times more reach.

Talking about brands: We were in the lucky situation that working for IBM we also could refer to them. Using brand names (when permitted) has a great effect on content. Even better is when you create original content with or about the brand – like we did here for IBM and a new study they had.

Dr. Robin Kiera @stratorob

#Cybersecurity: Being highly ranked isn't always good. 🛡️

According to @IBM 's Security X-Force Threat Intelligence Index 2023, the insurance and finance industry is the second most attacked by cybercriminals.

Even large organizations with professional
https://ibm.biz/XForceReport2023RK ......
pic.twitter.com/zMa7kr1KZ9

This also works when you curate news – like we did here with AWS – but original content is always better.

Dr. Robin Kiera @stratorob
#AWS announces new tools for building with #GenerativeAI

@AWS @ShellyKramer @StevenDickens3 @KirkDBorne
@lajacobsson @BettyK0 @EstelaMandela @bimedotcom
@dinisguarda @fogle_shane

#Cloud #BigData #AI #ML #DataScience

https://mb.com.ph/2023/4/17/aws-announces-new-tools-for-building-with-generative-ai ...

Reacting to Trends and Technology

For us, reacting to trends and technology has always worked well. It works even better when you not only talk about trends but actually provide orientation by answering the questions:

- Is it relevant?
- How does it matter to our industry?
- How does it matter to the viewer?
- What is *not* important about it?
- What are its flaws?

Tagging friends or people you know that could be interested in your content can also help.

Some of my posts with the biggest reach have been posts in which I humbly shared a recognition. If you provide a lot of value to your community and your industry and you then share that you achieve some recognition for it, the likelihood that a lot of people join in and also applaud you is great. From time to time people want to thank people who provide value. So my plea to you is: if you get a recognition please share it. This not only helps you but gives people the opportunity to say thank you. And I think we can use a thank you from time to time – as individuals, as industry, and as the human race.

Dr. Robin Kiera @stratorob

🚀 #ChatGPT is a game-changer in #AI technology, revolutionizing the way we interact with computers. How does it impact #fintech and #banking?

Check the thread below! 🧵
@SpirosMargaris @psb_dc @SabineVdL @guzmand @efipm @enricomolinari @albertogaruccio @FGraillot
pic.twitter.com/KtudpqIQSm

Dr. Robin Kiera @stratorob

🎉 Honored to be recognized by @belvo as a "Top 25 Fintech Influencer to Follow in 2023"! 🙌 Thanks to belvo for this inclusion - your contribution to finance and fintech is truly invaluable. 👏

🔗 Check out the list:
https://belvo.com/blog/fintech-influencers-and-newsletters-2023/ ...

Congrats to all! 🎊

#Fintech pic.twitter.com/rGBVBMTelA

Certain Days

The year is full of memorial and special days. If you produce content that relates to a specific day and the industry and maybe uses a little bit of humour, you can have success on social media and Twitter. A good example was my post on Valentine's Day. Why was it successful? We normally share industry news and content that is mostly quite serious – but me with a flower in my hand is quite unusual. Therefore people stopped their thumb sharing valuable (watch) time with us.

Dr. Robin Kiera @stratorob
Happy Heart's Day! Let's loosen up with some cheesy pick-up lines from the thread below. Don't leave me out in the cold, share yours in the comments. 💅

Any last-minute lines from you? 🖤
@DiklaWagner @tobiaskintzel @enilev @efipm

#ValentinesDay #Insurance #Finance
pic.twitter.com/xDTCu61tmQ

Events

People follow events on Twitter. Therefore, it makes sense to generate content about events. This helps your audience and the event organiser. For more ideas on how to use events please read Step 5 in this chapter.

Dr. Robin Kiera @stratorob
Congratulations Insurtech Insights for a
SOLD-OUT, record-breaking event! 🍾🎉
Excited to join the panel discussing "The
Race for GenZ - Optimizing your Distribution
for the Next Generation of Customers".

CC: @ipfconline1 @globaliqx @psb_dc
#Insurtech #GenZ #Insurance #Diversity
pic.twitter.com/8kA04gXDwH

Deutsche Familienversicherung – From 0 to 100

Before 2018, Deutsche Familienversicherung was almost unknown internationally. Elevating a medium-sized insurer from Frankfurt into the international arena, completely digitalising it, and successfully carrying out the first Insurtech IPO in the Western world was and is completely unrealistic. But DFV managed to do just that. Today, it is the number one listed Insurtech in Europe, and boasts huge achievements on its balance sheet and enormous customer growth.

This was driven by CEO and founder Dr Stefan Knoll and a team of insurance veterans and young employees. Dr Knoll set unrealistic goals – and achieved them in collaboration with his team.

Today, DFV is also internationally regarded as the exciting Insurtech case from Germany. DFV is even considered one of the best-case digital insurers alongside Lemonade, Ping An, and Zhong An in China.

All this was – when looked at objectively – completely unrealistic.

Interview with Lutz Kiesewetter, head of investor relations and corporate communications at DFV

How did you get to know Robin?

On social media, of course. Those who know him, know that everything is straightforward with him from the very first encounter. I wrote to him on LinkedIn and less than 24 hours later we spoke on the phone for the first time.

Why not have traditional agents?

We were in the middle of preparing a ground-breaking digital event, during which we wanted to position DFV as the first operating Insurtech. The event was scheduled for the 17th week of 2018 and was also to be documented on social media. As the PR manager, it was clear to me that we had to break new ground for this. Robin was already a force to be reckoned with in the international Insurtech community and was simply refreshingly different from all the other agents and experts. So he was an ideal partner for us.

What happened after the event and what were the focal points of the collaboration?

To be honest, before the collaboration continued, we first wanted to see whether his contributions and the first interview with Dr Knoll would have the anticipated impact. As it turned out, Robin delivers on his promises, so we extended our collaboration to include joint visits to international Insurtech trade fairs. It was easy to gain access using Robin's network. We were at DIA in Munich, Insurtech Connect in Las Vegas, and Insurtech Insights in London, to name a few events. Thanks to the interviews on site and Robin's dissemination on social media, awareness of DFV, especially internationally, further increased.

At the time, it was Europe's first Insurtech to go public.

What was Robin's role and what is your relationship like today?

After Robin had been intensively supporting DFV in the media for more than half a year, he was also on the trading floor on the day of the IPO. There was also another interview with Dr Knoll about the IPO. I think Robin was the ideal partner to support the first IPO of a European Insurtech in the media, as well as in the traditional media. Today, after the intense phase in 2018 and 2019, we still have a lot of contact and Robin has become a loyal DFV supporter. In the future, we will press ahead with joint projects.

Why is the book important for insurance practitioners?

I wish Robin every success with the book! As far as I know, there isn't a book on 'attention hacking' in the insurance industry yet, which is why, as a pioneer in this field, he can and will provide exciting insights that will be interesting far beyond the industry.

TikTok

If you're an insurer or agent and not on TikTok, you're missing out on the opportunity of the 2020s. TikTok is the hot platform as of March 2023. Don't worry about TikTok being notorious! The same was true for eBay, Facebook, and LinkedIn. Organic reach can still be achieved, so you should start NOW!

The network is used to create and share videos. Our account reaches up to 1,900,000 people per day and several million per week. In some instances, we are growing 10–20% a day. We do not make dance, travel, or comedy videos, but answer questions about assets, finance, and insurance. We are followed by 518,000 people and have gained over 15,900,000 likes so far.

We run TikTok accounts for various companies. As an agency we have become the market leader in the German insurance industry. We may not be able to talk about all of the channels we run, but to identify them is easy. Those who are successful are ours, those who are not . . . well, not. I know this sounds a little self-confident, but every TikTok channel we build up is successfully reaching millions and millions of people.

Our clients are the leaders in their markets on TikTok. The classical car insurer OCC, for example, which has about 100 employees and is a subsidiary of the huge insurer Provinzial, started its TikTok channel in 2021. After we took it over, we grew it from 3,000 to over 150,000 followers. From 2021 OCC reached millions and millions of customers and leads, for a fraction of the price of other channels.

Here are some facts about TikTok (per www.oberlo.com/ blog/tiktok-statistics,influencermarketinghub.com/tik tok-stats/):

- TikTok has over 1.5 billion active users worldwide and has been downloaded more than 3.5 billion times to date.
- Downloads have doubled in a year, making TikTok one of the fastest-growing social networks in the world.
- Contrary to public perception, only 41% of users are between 16 and 24 years old, and TikTok is increasingly engaging older people. Over 40% of users are aged over 25.
- Users spend an average of 95 minutes per day on TikTok – this length of time beats all other apps.
- TikTok is available in 155 countries and 75 languages.
- Most other apps are only used once a day, but 90% of users are on TikTok multiple times a day.

Here are your first steps:

1. Work out a TikTok strategy now, in 5 years it will be too late.
2. Rid yourself of everything you've heard about TikTok in the media, from self-proclaimed experts or colleagues. Make up your own mind.
3. Create your own profile and like content that you find exciting. Then the algorithm will learn to provide you with relevant content.
4. Consistently analyse what you like and why certain videos are successful.
5. Research hashtags and topics you want to cover.
6. Start your own channel and publish videos that are suitable for TikTok!

7. Make sure TikTok users can find your profile on other portals, such as LinkedIn, and boost your followers there, too. Link-Tree is a good option to do this. You can use a link to refer to an external page, where in turn several links to the other profiles can be provided.

8. If you feel comfortable and confident, create lots of TikTok videos daily. Ideally between 20 and 40.

Content That Works on TikTok

It is impossible to predict the success of a video on TikTok in advance, although principles are emerging that contribute to how viral it will go. So use trial and error to get better acquainted with these principles! We were able to gain a lot of views with financial, car, and travel videos, for example, which offer numerous opportunities for bringing up insurance topics. We also get good viewer numbers with more serious financial tips, especially in contrast to channels that propagate senseless consumption and 'flexing' (displaying status symbols).

Insurance topics are also well suited to short TikTok videos. Briefly edit your day in the agent's office or show a customer's new and well-insured car and briefly explain what is involved.

Here are some dos and don'ts

- Never share videos produced for other channels such as YouTube or LinkedIn. TikTok has its own set of rules. Only TikTok-specific content has the potential to go viral.
- Videos that provide entertainment, information, and practical help are well received.
- Motivational and positive videos are well received, negative ones are not.

- Block haters rigorously and do not get embroiled in any arguments.
- Videos should be between 15 and 60 seconds long.

Here are some pro tips:

- TikTok also offers a live streaming function. Unlike the majority of other channels, you can also reach people who do not yet follow you.
- Start videos with strong messages or the most important words. With TikTok, you have half a second to a second to get people's attention.
- Try out different types of content. It is almost impossible to guess which topics will gain traction in advance. We actually wanted to start a consulting channel, but our videos on finance and wealth were so successful that we changed our minds completely.
- Adapt current trending hashtags and topics to your field.
- Populate hashtags by creating lots of videos about them. If these go viral, you can carve out entire niches, like we did with #WealthBuilding.
- Consider collaborating with other influencers.
- The advertising feature is still new and unproven, but check out the potential it offers.
- If you're not investing in TikTok now, then read this book from the beginning again.

Must-Watch Channels

Here are some must-watch channels:

- Herr Anwalt
- Cosmosdirekt
- Wuerth_Germany

- canderkoch
- PolizeiNRW
- dfv.ag
- Echt OCC
- Nikolas Kolorz
- aditotoro
- Footdocdana
- steuerfabi
- Idea.Soup
- Zach King
- Midovibes
- versicherungenmitkopf

You can also follow my channel: Robin_Kiera

 **robin_kiera** ✓

Attention Hacker

☑ **Edit profile**

1631 Following   **518.7K** Followers   **15.9M** Likes

CEO of Diggi. Unternehmer. 💚 Immobilien. Eure virale Social Media Agentur

🔗 Www.linktr.ee/Robin.kiera

Strategies That We've Used

Knowledge and Relatable Situations

We run channels for insurers, banks, and ourselves that focus on finance, real estate, and financial literacy. Therefore, a lot of the topics we talk about are not part of the daily lives of most people on social media – at first glance.

It is important to provide content that sends across the message of complex topics, products, and services but also connects with the everyday life of people. Therefore, we combine topics such as: evaluation of real estate with things people can relate to, even if they don't own real estate.

In the following example we ask whether the bus stop in front of the house has an effect on the value of the real estate. Even though you may not own a home, you surely (at least in most parts of the world) have used public transportation and know bus stops. Therefore with this video we combine wider topics with our niche core to address more people.

#ceoofdiggi #teamdiggi ...

Interview Situations

A lot of content can be shot as an interview situation. So you can develop topics and then rapidly shoot interviews. The secret is that you need to limit your statement to one good point; it can be a surprising thesis, statistic, or claim. The more controversial or personal, generally the more reach. I once 'revealed' the balance of my bank account. A lot of viewers expected a high balance, but it was not. I shot the video to make the point that money needs to be invested not left lying around.

Kontostand REVEAL!!!! ...

There was a similar video in which I shared that I actually drive a pretty old car. In this video I wanted to make the point that if you want to build wealth you should invest your money and not drive a fancy car that decreases in value. Companies can also play with these surprising facts.

Hättet ihr das gedacht? ...

Role Play

A strategy that worked well included role play alongside telling and showing about the selected topic. We used different approaches. We filmed two different Robins with different clothes on playing different types of people – for example a real estate owner and a renter or a rich person and a really rich person.

#ceoofdiggi #teamdiggi ...

It can also make sense to combine role playing with situations in everyday life – for example, when your credit card gets declined (see the following shot from a video). Feel free to also exaggerate playing different roles to underline the point you want to make.

Everyday Situations

It makes sense to comment on everyday situations to illustrate your overall points and topics. Here, for example, I underlined the fate of physical stores against online shops as a result of queueing.

#deutschland #ceoofdiggi...

Wenn man schon mal hing...

Sharing Knowledge

On our channel we don't dance or do questionable things to get views, we provide information to try to educate the audience (as we recommend most companies should do too). Sharing knowledge in a relatable way is the way to go. This can be done in front of a white board or outside showing the things you talk about (for example, real estate). In the video (see the following shots) we talk about the three signs when not to buy a multifamily home. Warnings and things *not* to do work way better than positive tips. That is a weird finding but it is what it is.

#ceoofdiggi #teamdiggi ...

#ceoofdiggi #teamdiggi ...

Facts and Figures

It can also work to share facts and figures – but to put them into a situation that people can relate to. So show how much money Elon Musk has and show that a regular person saving US$500 per month would need to save for 45 million years. That video (screen shot follows) went quite viral and had a lengthy discussion because it combined interesting data, a celebrity, and a new insight. Companies also could use interesting industry or product data to get the attention of their clients.

#musk #tesla #elonmusk ...

Outing Scammers

On TikTok there are sometimes people that try to scam others or to pretend to be something that they are not. The latter is totally fine as long as they don't try to rip people off. Particularly at the beginning of my TikTok career I felt obliged to warn the (back then) mostly young people about shady sales organisations or dubious people with online courses. Outing scammers always went very well, but only because I researched a lot to arrive at my opinion and had data to back my claims.

For companies, this is a category I might not pursue, because it is a quite negative category. I personally skip 9 out of 10 opportunities because it's a negative sort of content, but on the other hand I feel obliged to spread awareness and help younger people on the platform.

Disclaimer: ich wurde 2011 ...   Prüft die Qualifikation und ...   #blender fliegen irgendwa...

Luxury Can Work

Despite the fact that most people can't afford luxury items, showing and using them – the more expensive the better – can reach a lot of people. Why? Because they want to see how 'rich' people live. Let us not forget that on social media that is used by masses of people different standards apply than, for example, on LinkedIn.

When I flew to the Philippines to visit our office there, I took my daughter with me. And I shared, on TikTok, one small detail (of not having children's food for a €6,000 ticket). This and other flying business class videos went quite viral. A lot of people discussed if it is worth the extra money, particularly as you don't arrive any earlier. For us it was a business trip and the sleep was worth the difference between a regular and a business class ticket.

#ceoofdiggi #teamdiggi ...

Influencing Can Work

We regularly visit and interview influencers with a much larger following, such as Jeremy Fragrance. But we noted with our influencer interviews that only those videos and influencers that were close to our core topics really worked. We had interviews with super famous people with millions of followers but with only limited views per video, because their core topic was far away from our core topic.

Investerit ihr in Aktien und ...

An influencer that worked quite well on our channel was Mark Gebauer, who built a US$40+ million business based on luxury watches. So his audience was similar to but not the same as mine (focusing on real estate and finances). We had a 45-minute interview and we cut the best scenes to various small micro interviews and published them on various channels including TikTok where it worked quite well. Companies also could regularly talk to influencers or celebrities in a fun way.

#uhren vs #immobilien ...

Facebook

In my experience, Facebook is dead as a platform for attention hacking. Posts no longer get much organic reach and no one reads them. You rarely reach your target groups on Facebook. Exceptions to this are some groups for agents or brokers, or extremely active communities in groups. However, it makes sense to post content from other platforms on Facebook as well.

I cannot and will not give you step-by-step instructions for your Facebook account here now. Even I was years too late in building a community there. Only advertising opportunities may be of interest to you. From online gaming to insurance, various industries generate leads through Facebook advertising.

Pro tricks

- Check whether Facebook demographic groups that are of interest to you can be specifically narrowed down.
- Sometimes targeted advertising can be placed within a radius of 500 metres of an agent's office.
- Facebook is suitable for secondary or tertiary use of content.
- For example, you can automatically integrate livestreams for other platforms on Facebook using interfaces.

Instagram

This platform quickly raises the fundamental question: can you really sell on Instagram? The answer is yes. It is true that a lot of people just want to see nice images or post great photos of their latest holiday. Beyond that, however, Instagram has evolved to become a knowledge platform. In our case, (insurance) information combined with personal stories and content can build the necessary trust amongst customers. Those who provide their content within the platform framework can also gain insurance customers on Instagram without adverts.

Data and facts about Instagram (per `www.blog.hoot` `suite.com/instagram-statistics/`, `https://www.oberlo.` `de/blog/instagram-statistik`):

- 2.9 billion people use Instagram every month.
- In Germany, Instagram has around 30 million users.
- The largest user group is comprised of 25–34 year olds.
- 59% of users log in at least once a day.
- Users spend an average of 53 minutes per day on the platform.
- 50% of users follow at least one business site.
- A third of the most-viewed stories come from companies.
- Brands post an average of 2.5 stories each week.

Here are your first steps:

1. Get an accurate overview of the content on Instagram that is relevant to your topic area.
2. Think of a good reason why other people should follow you.
3. Look to see which users you can network with.
4. Think about how your expertise can be represented graphically and how it can be showcased on Instagram.

Content That Works on Instagram

It goes without saying that you will have to adapt your content to the platform. Be creative! Create posts that are beautiful to look at and deliver value or entertainment. You can use Instagram to provide insights into your business. After all, virtually no one knows what goes on behind the closed doors of an insurer or agent's office. In this way, you make the industry appear more human and approachable. Why don't you let the interns have a go at it to start with or get professionals on board to reach the next level?

Dos and don'ts

- Always be present on Instagram and make sure you have regular posts that are not about the company.
- Focus on the wishes, needs, and interests of your target group.
- Act more relaxed and easygoing than is expected from an insurer or agent.
- Don't misunderstand Instagram as an advertising space! Those who only post adverts are guaranteed not to succeed organically. It may make sense to try out advertising products, but make sure to differentiate between delivering organic value and hardcore selling in adverts. Never annoy your audience with advertising too much. You should deliver 80–90% value and advertise only 10–20% maximum.
- Make content easy to understand.

Instead of telling you about Instagram myself, I asked the most successful insurance broker in Germany on there – Bastian Kunkel:

On Instagram, it's like any other social media platform, I have to give potential new customers a reason to follow or interact with me. That is classic added value. This approach has nothing to do with the usual push marketing, 'pull' is the key here. I don't act as a salesperson and post my phone number everywhere. Instead, I act as a friendly helper from next door and share my knowledge without a hidden agenda.

Instagram is not an advertising space that you can plaster with your adverts. Unfortunately, many colleagues do exactly that and then wonder why they don't attract customers on Instagram. I regularly post articles that talk about insurance. My stories provide personal insights into my life as an insurance broker so that followers can better envision the whole experience. Only now and then do I indirectly mention free online advice.

Sometimes I even make money from Instagram by repeatedly running campaigns as an influencer and getting paid for my reach. This, however, is only on the side. But a lot of work is needed before that can happen. Instagram is not a hobby or something you can do on the side. It needs a strategy, the right positioning and excellent content. I have to deliver added value instead of awkward advertising messages. And, of course, share stories about everyday life with my followers. And perhaps the most important thing is consistency. If you don't stick with it, you might as well drop it.

Other Channels

You have now seen the main channels; here are a couple more.

Podcasts

Audio tracks of videos can be used as sound files, given an introduction and credits, and then distributed as an independent medium. We use a service called Anchor (www .anchor.fm), but Spotify is also useful. Additionally, you can include podcasts in your web offering or refer to them with the help of email distribution.

Email Newsletters

Individual framework conditions dictate whether you seek the attention of your target group regularly via newsletter, for example, once or twice a week or monthly. This method can be useful if you have an extensive mailing list and content can be reused without the need for additional effort. For example, you can promote highlights from other platforms via newsletters, but you should tailor them to the target audience.

A new trend we see in the United States and the United Kingdom is VIP Newsletters. They are sent to a small group of close supporters, customers, and friends. The content is purely high value and provides exclusive information or comments on industry trends and news. We also include personal information about our company and – maybe – sensitive information on our strategy and plans. The result: a lot of decision-makers are increasing their support for our firm and we deliver true value.

Chapter 13

Become
a Content Machine

The average person is bombarded with approximately 10,000 advertising messages each day. Given this sheer volume, anyone who sends out a monthly newsletter or a letter once a year might as well not bother at all. It simply vanishes. Only those who are always visible will be listened to. Whether it's videos, tweets, blog posts, or other content, those who miss the mark waste resources unnecessarily and are quickly forgotten. While high-quality content with real added value does matter, the most important advice for successful attention hacking, in my opinion, is do more!

While a few years ago you could still garner attention with a few videos and images, today there is intense competition for target groups. Anyone who has been able to achieve status as an important influencer has a big head start. With the required effort, however, even newcomers can earn this kind of status – with the required effort. Some people in the insurance industry are also waiting to mock people with fresh ideas. Ignore such negative influences as best you can!

Even if I am labouring the point here, attention can only be garnered with valuable content – customers have to get something out of it. Your content or app must solve a customer problem – for free. Think of a successful app like WhatsApp. Anyone who predicted 10 years ago that you would get accessible real-time communication world-wide for free would have been laughed at. However, the insurance industry must also internalise this value concept, especially since it has the ideal prerequisites. For example, insurers are absolute experts on physical and financial well-being thanks to their customer data. Use this gem and share it with people! You can then sell as a second step.

Don't Get Fleeced

Forget the glossy video once a year that your marketing agency likes to charge US$150,000 to 1,500,000 for. Design awards are mainly of interest to the advertising industry; your customers have nothing to gain from them! Success on social media comes down to the quantity of content published, not the graphic quality. Therefore, one of your most important tasks is to create material on a conveyor belt.

All matters, events, dates, and many external factors facilitate the production of corresponding images, videos, or posts. You can achieve the required click rate by using an event several times. Give a speech and produce a long format. Edit several short videos from it and write different texts on the respective key points. A 'making of' video can usually also be created.

Whenever I speak with industry leaders about this tool, there is a question that always comes up: when can we put a price on this valuable content? My answer is never! You would immediately be showing yourself the red card. Even Google and Facebook would never think of putting their services behind payment barriers. Instead, the successful tech giants provide user-friendly services to garner attention and infiltrate people's daily routines. They are the kings of attention hacking! Then they act as the man in the middle or the gatekeeper and earn their (outrageous amount of) money by providing access to others, such as insurers. Every manager in the car industry has a mixture of pain and anger when thinking about the budgets that insurers keep transferring to these gatekeepers at the end of the year when trying to win new customers. Such a development should be avoided in the future.

Being a Content Machine

These are the five parts of a successful content machine:

1. Establish the conditions for content creation.

   As a beginner, you need a camera, hardware, and software to edit videos, sound, and graphics, as well as human resources. In the beginning, an up-to-date mobile phone will do at a pinch. Content creators need dedicated time and an adapted job description. When you want to become a content champion – especially as a mid-size or larger company – you need to get professionals on board. When you want to win the super bowl or the champions league make sure to get the best players and coaches on board.

2. Create good content!

Test out different options and follow the strategy that works. If you find yourself asking at this point, 'Kiera, what is good content?', then read the relevant chapters again or contact us.

3. Publish good content on third-party channels.

The ultimate discipline is to place your own content with media partners. You will benefit from their reach and gain new fans.

4. Become a content platform.

Invite others to participate in your content formats, as we do in our Insurance and Finance Live series with the who's who of the international insurance industry.

5. Set up a professional sales funnel.

If you discover interesting people among your followers, why not move into a sales process? Or why not invite interesting people into their own segment and become active in distribution?

How to Achieve a High Click Rate

You can build a real content machine. The trick is to produce core content – like a high-quality video or video interview – and then edit and reuse it in a way that is suitable for the channel.

For example, in the case of an interview, you have the video-recorded interview as core content. The audio track can be edited into a podcast. A generic intro and outro can be added, and it can be shared on distribution platforms. That's done. You can prepare the best quotes as graphics and share them. You can usually cut between 5 and 15 highlights out of a 30-minute interview.

A summary video is also an option. Furthermore, critical statements can also be displayed in text form, and relevant articles can be written in multiple languages. The best way is to publish them in recognised specialist media. If you follow this principle consistently, you can implement an entire campaign from manageable core content and use it to establish a presence on all relevant channels with high-quality and specific content. This way, you can produce and disseminate at least 10 times more content with your current budget than you do today.

Create Quantity and Publish Quality

I would like to repeat the most important principle in this chapter: start now! Those who do not have the necessary resources in-house should call in external experts. This eliminates the time spent testing things out, and success can be achieved much more quickly.

I'm Just a Broker, How Am I Supposed to Do That?

Not everyone can recruit 5 or 10 people for social media or hire a leading social media agency. However, with the technology available on smartphones, you can do a lot yourself. If you want to survive change, you have to spend time on it. Change your focus and focus on the strategies of tomorrow! The work of the industry is changing. You may even have experts who can do the necessary activities instead of annoying customers with cold calls.

Chapter 14
Identify Your Relevant Influencers

Insurance companies, agents, employed sales managers, and other industry players garner attention on the basis of engagement. Get active! To do this, it is best to start with the important influencers and multipliers.

First you'll want to identify the people who are important; you should be kind to other people; and you should help other people. You'll find that if you help others that they will help you.

Identify People Who Are Important to You

The first step is to identify people who are important to you. For example, Google #insurance and you'll come across people and companies who are active on a regular basis. There are also rankings for players in the Fintech and Insurtech sectors. Be on the lookout for decision-makers.

The key community for your objectives can be global, national, regional, or local. For example, as an agent in the region, look at who is in your city and target industries active on social media. In a nutshell, do some searching! There is a certain amount of research required, especially at the beginning. But after that, you will know the people playing key roles in your field and whose support is important to you. If the relevant actors are known, you can engage in active communication.

Be Kind to Others

Endorse, share, or like other people's posts that you like. This way, influencers and decision-makers will eventually take notice of you, and the chances of you getting support for your business will increase. Always remember that the other influencers want to help. So engage with them and other members because they are often consumers and, as a result, potential customers.

You should also like, comment on, and share their posts. Sometimes questions come up that you can answer with your expertise. This positions you as a trustworthy expert. However, it is always important to be positive. You should also always respond to criticism in a constructive and respectful way. Offer solutions and not arguments.

Help Others and You Will Receive Help

The people you engage with usually react positively if you make yourself known with likes and positive comments. You will quickly succeed in gaining an influencer as an interview partner or something similar. In this way, you will benefit from the reach of others and ultimately become an important figure on social media yourself – in other words, an influencer!

Chapter 15

Build Social Media into Your Daily Routine

Everyone knows that if you don't exercise regularly, you won't improve or even maintain your health. If you want to be at the top of the game, you have to put a lot of effort into it. Even more so, successful athletes align their daily life with their sports. Really good athletes do it with a smile.

When Arnold Schwarzenegger was once asked in the gym at the beginning of his career why he smiled while other professional athletes groaned, he replied that he looked forward to every set of 50 push-ups – even if it hurt. That ultimately brought him closer to his goal of becoming Mr Universe. To be successful on social media, you need to look forward to the next video and selfie as much as Arnold Schwarzenegger looked forward to his next exercise routine.

If you want to garner attention in marketing, as an agent, manager, or board member, you need to integrate attention hacking into your daily routine. Here are some tips:

- Set fixed social media times every day. During the set-up phase, my TikTok plan looked like this:
  - 7:00 to 8:30 a.m.: Family time
  - 8:30 a.m.: Arrive at the office
  - 8:30 to 10:00 a.m.: Record and produce TikTok videos
  - 10:00 a.m. to 6:00 p.m.: Regular work
  - 6:00 to 8:00 p.m.: Family time
  - 8:00 to 9:00 p.m. (2–3 times a week): Livestreaming
- Create routines for producing and publishing content.
- Block out the required time in your calendar.
- Involve your colleagues and hold regular planning and review meetings.
- Check every activity and every event for links to posts.

Chapter 16
Build an Effective Sales Funnel

Attention hacking is not an end in itself; newly acquired contacts should facilitate additional business success in the future. Although you might get leads from Twitter, YouTube, and the like, a structured funnel is needed. Whether it's about new customers, potential employees, or interesting partners, you have to channel the respective contacts and manage the follow-up. The answer to the following question highlights the focus: What should I do with my new contacts?

Create a detailed plan of when you will do what. For example, I thank a new contact immediately after a meeting or similar via WhatsApp, and I usually send an email follow-up on the same day. If nothing happens, I follow up after three days. If it is practical where physical products are involved, I also send these off immediately. Basically, it's about increasing the number of contact points. Establish a routine of what you do on day one, day two, day five, and so on. As always in the context of social media, friendliness and authenticity matter. Avoid impersonal mass emails!

Whenever you make contact, remember that it's not about selling. It is all about helping people. This approach must be apparent in all your communication. Only then will contacts voluntarily approach you when they need something. Only then will attention turn into trust. You literally build a social network.

You will quickly notice that attention hacking generates a lot of contacts. Therefore, it makes sense to partially automate the sales funnel. Templates, scheduled calls, automated messages, and structured processes are all useful tools. Even with a small team, a big impact can be achieved.

Building a structured sales funnel with systematic and planned touchpoints deserves a book of its own. If this book is successful and readers like you pass it on to your fellow insurance professionals, I'll write about that, too.

Now you know the 10 steps you need to follow to be successful at attention hacking. You may have even shaken your head in disbelief that it really can be that simple. My experience shows that you will certainly succeed with the steps I have outlined. So, yes – it's that simple! What is not easy is actually doing it. Remember that it took me 7 years. Doubts, hesitations, and excuses slowed me down. Do better! Take advantage of my experience and take the first step right away. If you lack the resources or experience other hurdles, there is a solution for that, too – find support. Even if you could guarantee it, you don't have to do everything yourself!

Despite the fact that beginning by yourself is simple – especially after you read the whole book – it is important to remember that if you really want to be the best and most effective and efficient person or company to hack the attention of your target group you must master the conceptualising, producing, and managing of content and communities. To achieve this yourself is possible – but it takes a long time. It is better to get the best with you on board. Our clients have saved years and made millions and millions more by taking a shortcut, getting access to our knowledge and our content machine.

Get Experts

It's unusual for someone to become an influencer overnight. In the finance and insurance sector in particular, it takes years to gain the necessary trust of other users. Only where such a relationship exists can social contacts be transformed into real business. Therefore, the same applies to attention hacking in most other areas. If extremely specialised expertise is required, you should consider outsourcing. The motto is: get on the fast track to becoming an influencer!

In my experience, it makes sense to include experts in your activities.

This principle not only reduces the workload, it also allows a large unit of reliable employees to be built up. However, it takes years to get the right team in place. Expect to have to experiment a lot! However, once it is in place, you have a robust and scalable tool for your projects. Tasks are completed quickly and with a high level of quality, and it is possible to actively shape the change in target groups and technologies. This opportunity exists no matter the size of your company! Regardless of whether you are an agent, agency, sales manager, or insurer, you always have the right staff at your disposal!

Some of our clients hire us because they have great marketing teams – but not for social media or attention hacking. Sometimes these departments think first and foremost in terms of beautiful brochures, well laid-out advertisements or expensive films. They're great at all of that. However, very few have effective social media campaigns up their sleeves. People spend money on Facebook and the like, but the effect stays at zero. This is one of the reasons why most CEOs, for example, do not have their own followers. So I have two key criticisms:

- For a lot of money, agencies deliver things that are long outdated.
- Agencies do not run their own successful channels.

Without their own successful brand, followers or social media presence, how can marketing agencies credibly claim they can provide these services to our industry? You don't need a zookeeper to survive in the digital jungle, you need Crocodile Dundee.

Wasting money and unrealistic strategies can be avoided by those who are active in the social media world and know the dos and don'ts. I had to experience this for myself and the current success of Digitalscouting and our clients is based on 10 years of work. It is also based on the ability to react very quickly to new developments. Especially in fast-moving areas like social networks, the combination of expertise and speed is essential. Unfortunately, the insurance industry often lacks both.

From my point of view, it may be useful to outsource many activities related to attention hacking to someone who has a proven track record in it. This avoids the time-consuming process of setting up corresponding teams and shortens lengthy decision-making processes in the company. This also helps you to reach the next level quicker and makes it more likely to get to the top. Rely on external specialists with proven expertise in this area! In this case, you will see your marketing department quickly grow by 30 social media experts.

Outsourcing allows you to start overtaking overnight. You will attract people who place thousands of videos or posts every year in a wide variety of channels and reach large target groups. Take Digitalscouting, for example. We usually reach millions of people in a niche area like insurance. Innovative outsourcing also helps to avoid the typical beginner's mistakes. So my advice is that you outsource to us.

Now Is Your Chance!

Congratulations, now you have all the information you need and have learned plenty of tricks to position sales and marketing for the present and the future.

Chapter 17
Summing Up Attention Hacking

I n this chapter, I will summarise once again why you should start now and what you should do.

- People change! And so do the means of communication, preferences and viewing habits. Whether you like this or not, you have to respond. If you don't, sooner or later you'll end up like Kodak and Toys 'R' Us.
- Insurance sales no longer work! Many people do not like your approach, even if you are currently earning a reasonable amount of money. If other players develop better initiatives, your business will migrate to the competition.
- People are social creatures, which is why social media works so well. Take advantage of this principle and reallocate your resources accordingly. Would you still buy a telex device?
- Today, attention is what matters! Amid enormous sensory overload, it is crucial that you get noticed. So, do

everything you can to gain the attention of your target groups. Become an influencer.

- After all, it is mainly the trusted service providers that people remember. Earn that trust by offering help. Listen up! Then, if you know your target groups, you should use your extensive knowledge of security and assets!
- You will only succeed if you get a high click rate. Forget about expensive adverts and instead be on your customers' smartphone when they look at it during ad breaks.
- Change your sales and marketing strategy! Integrate communication with your target groups into your daily routine and be present where people are at the moment. You don't like channel XY? You want to sell, right?
- Get started right away, time is short! If in-house resources are lacking, outsource! At Digitalscouting, we can get you started right away.

Do you have concerns because your company does not (yet) meet the requirements? Don't wait for all the old problems to be solved. That will never happen. Always remember that problems never stop cropping up. There are always new ones! But where 10 difficulties arise, you will celebrate 20 successes!

Two Scenarios for the Future of Insurers

Here are two scenarios for the future of the industry. Which do you want to be?

- The bad companies prevail, and there is no innovation. The industry continues to work with outdated concepts and spends its time arguing about why new things can't work. The result is that others will gain more and more market share and profits will continue to shrink. Many insurers end up like Kodak and Polaroid.

- The good companies prevail thanks to implementing the modern and successful concepts discussed in this book. Ideas from smaller companies flow into the mix, and the industry expands its value chain. On the whole, we are moving closer to the customer. The result is that a new, golden age can commence, and the insurance industry occupies the place in society that it is capable of filling by virtue of its capabilities.

Chapter 18

Digitalscouting: We Make Your Customer Come to You

We are a European-Asian marketing agency – one of the leading in the central European insurance industry. We are not a social media service provider that produces colourful images and makes cool videos. No, what we do is increase our clients' likelihood of success. Although we cost money, this investment is recouped at least 10-fold. What are €500,000 in expenses for *xx* million in additional turnover?

You should also choose us as a partner because you would need 5 to 10 years to be able to implement the necessary strategies on your own. As knowledge sharing and relationships are based on the attention garnered from customers and partners, you have to work at it. I know this challenge from my own experience and our clients, and this book is the culmination of my 10+ years in social media.

For example, it is fed by the generation of millions of leads for our customers.

There are also copycats and free riders in the market, and they are usually less expensive than Digitalscouting. However, the knowledge gained from dozens of projects, tens of thousands of posts, thousands of videos, and over 250 million views is what sets us apart. Sure, you can copy one or two aspects of attention hacking, but not the knowledge and experience, and definitely not the network and not our 30+ people team in Europe and Asia!

Digitalscouting supports companies in four main areas:

- We audit and review your marketing, social media, and sales strategy and process. We deliver a detailed plan, to get you closer to your customer.
- We implement your sales, marketing, and social media strategy – it might be as sparring partner or as fully fledged outsourced marketing department.
- We take over the setup of your LinkedIn, Twitter, YouTube, Instagram, and TikTok accounts and manage your VIP Newsletter.
- We produce the most viral videos of the industry – from social media to premium TV campaigns.

Get Started – With Us

Great, you did it! You are not burying your head in the sand like so many others. That is why I am quite sure that your company will be one of the winners. Those who face the facts have already won. This is miles ahead of most of the competition. Your ability to recognise the reality of the situation shows that you are ready to get started and move your business forward. With this attitude as well as the willingness to change, you are sure to get through to your customers. You will garner attention.

We are happy to support you in this endeavour to help you reach your goals faster.

Just Drop Me a Line

If you could do with some good karma, close your eyes, think of three people who need to read this book, and gift it to them now on Amazon. Your friends will thank you.

Index